THE COLD WAR, JOE McCARTHY, AND THE RED SCARE

WITCH HUNT

ANDREA BALIS
ELIZABETH LEVY

ILLUSTRATIONS BY
TIM FOLEY

ROARING BROOK PRESS
NEW YORK

Published by Roaring Brook Press
Roaring Brook Press is a division of Holtzbrinck Publishing Holdings Limited Partnership
120 Broadway, New York, NY 10271 • mackids.com

Our books may be purchased in bulk for promotional, educational, or business use. Please contact your local bookseller or the Macmillan Corporate and Premium Sales Department at (800) 221-7945 ext. 5442 or by email at MacmillanSpecialMarkets@macmillan.com.

Library of Congress Cataloging-in-Publication Data
Names: Balis, Andrea, author. | Levy, Elizabeth, 1942– author. |
Foley, Tim, 1962– illustrator.
Title: Witch hunt : the Cold War, Joe McCarthy, and the Red Scare / Andrea Balis & Elizabeth Levy ; illustrations by Tim Foley.
Other titles: Cold War, Joe McCarthy, and the Red Scare
Description: First edition. | New York : Roaring Brook Press, 2024. | Includes bibliographical references and index. | Audience: Ages 10–14 | Audience: Grades 7–9
Summary: "A cutting-edge look into a pivotal moment in U.S. history: McCarthy's infamous 'witch hunt' for communists during the 1950's Red Scare." —Provided by publisher.
Identifiers: LCCN 2023013500 | ISBN 9781250246813 (hardcover) | ISBN 9781250246820 (ebook)
Subjects: LCSH: Anti-communist movements—United States—History—20th century—Juvenile literature. | McCarthy, Joseph, 1908–1957—Juvenile literature. | United States. Congress. House. Committee on Un-American Activities—Juvenile literature. | Subversive activities—United States—History—20th century—Juvenile literature. | Cold War—Juvenile literature. | United States—Politics and government—20th century—Juvenile literature.
Classification: LCC E743.5 .B255 2024 | DDC 973.9—dc23/eng/20230607
LC record available at https://lccn.loc.gov/2023013500

First edition, 2024
Book design by L. Whitt
Printed in the United States of America by Lakeside Book Company, Harrisonburg, Virginia

ISBN 978-1-250-24681-3

1 3 5 7 9 10 8 6 4 2

TO OUR PARENTS, BERNICE AND EARL BALIS
AND MILDRED AND ELMER LEVY, AND OUR
SIBLINGS, LAWRENCE LEVY AND ELLEN BALIS

CONTENTS

AUTHOR'S NOTE

People often say they wish they could have been a fly on the wall during various historical events, as if that way they would get the "inside story" of what really happened. That's because they would like to witness what unfolded firsthand. But there is not just one inside story, and new facts and sources are frequently being uncovered. The way we see the past is shaped by the present, and the present keeps on changing.

Historians decide themselves when to begin the story, when to end it, what to include and what to leave out, even how to phrase or summarize events. Sometimes it's hard to know which is the "real" fact. Sometimes seemingly contradictory facts are all true. We wanted to tell the story of Joseph McCarthy and the Red Scare through the words of the people directly involved. We included footnotes so that you, the reader, can learn more about what you're studying. Of course, different sources can report the same events slightly differently. People can lie or change their story. So in telling the full arc of the story, we occasionally had to exercise some editorial judgment in ordering or relaying what people said when—but we did so minimally and with an eye on the larger historical frame.

History is stories. The details have meaning when you have a story to connect them. By looking back, we can get a more complicated understanding of our own world, just as we often understand our own actions differently when we look back on them. We both lived through the 1950s, the time we are writing about here. We knew people whose families were deeply affected by the Red Scare. The families and friends of people who make headlines are not often counted or named in history books, but they are a kind of collateral damage, and as much a part of history as the main event. We had them in mind as we wrote this book.

—Andrea Balis and Elizabeth Levy, 2024

INTRODUCTION
ROBIN HOOD, WITCHES, AND COMMIES

NEWSPAPER ARTICLE: Indiana Censor Fears Little Red Robin Hood: "Robin Hood robbed the rich and gave it to the poor. That's the Communist line."

FLY ON THE WALL: In the 1950s, one person on the Indiana Textbook Commission tried to bar kids from reading about Robin Hood because she thought he might turn them into communists.

Robin Hood is the legendary folk hero from the Middle Ages who stood up for the poor. Along with Robin Hood, witches were also a legend in medieval times. Almost everything that went wrong was blamed on witches. If you were named a witch, there was really no way to prove your innocence. One test was to be dropped into the village pond with a stone tied to your body. If you sank and drowned, you were not a witch. If you floated to the top, you were a witch and then you were burned.

There was no way out.

VEENA PATEL, HISTORIAN: The ordeal of the swimming test originated as an old Germanic rite and . . . usually involved the tying of a suspect's wrists to their ankles and then throwing the individual into a body of water . . . If the suspect sank, they were presumed innocent and hauled up . . . Should they float, however, this was taken as confirmation of their alliance with the Devil.

FLY ON THE WALL: This book is about another kind of witch hunt: the hunt for communists in the middle of the twentieth century. Communism is a political philosophy that was defined in 1848 in a pamphlet called *The Communist Manifesto* by Karl Marx and Friedrich Engels. When Marx and Engels wrote their pamphlet, factories were spreading in Europe and the United States, and working conditions were horrible. As Marx and Engels put it, the owners of the factories saw workers as parts of their new machines and not as people. The communists felt that since the people in the factories were doing the actual work, they should be getting the actual profits.

THE COMMUNIST MANIFESTO (1848): Let the ruling classes tremble at a Communistic revolution.

FLY ON THE WALL: It was *The Communist Manifesto* that so frightened factory owners. They thought that since they had risked money to build factories, all the profits belonged to them. Russia saw political and social revolutions in 1917. Some of the leaders were in part inspired by the *Communist Manifesto*, calling for the workers to revolt.

THE COMMUNIST MANIFESTO: Workers of all countries, unite!

FLY ON THE WALL: The czar was overthrown, and eventually he and his entire family were executed. The American public was scared that the communist revolution in Russia might spread to the United States.

DR. JOHN WESLEY HILL, METHODIST MINISTER: If I were to deport bolshevists I would have a ship of stone with sails of lead.

FLY ON THE WALL: By the middle of the twentieth century, the world was locked in what was known as the Cold War. On one side were the world's democracies led by the United States, including France, Britain, and Australia. Against them was the communist world led by the Soviet Union, which was made up of Russia and the many countries under its control, like Ukraine, Latvia, Estonia, and Lithuania. Aligned with Russia were other communist countries such as Poland and Czechoslovakia. The fight against communism in the 1940s and 1950s became known as the Red Scare. The color red became associated with rebels and rebellion against government, especially after an uprising in Paris in 1870.

> **KARL MARX:** The old world writhed in convulsions of rage at the sight of the Red Flag, the symbol of the Republic of Labor.

> **THE ALL-RUSSIAN CENTRAL EXECUTIVE COMMITTEE, APRIL 14, 1918:** The flag of the Russian Republic is to be the red banner with the following inscription: the Russian Soviet Federative Socialist Republic.

FLY ON THE WALL: Americans were so afraid of communists, or Reds, living among them that they began to hunt them like witches. These witches were called "commies, pinkos, un-American." And that's why there was a call to ban Robin Hood.

> **LIBRARIAN:** How does one prove one isn't a Communist?

> **LIBRARIAN:** I wish I could tell.

FLY ON THE WALL: During the Red Scare, it soon became clear that, as with accused witches, the only way to float to the top of the pond and save yourself was to accuse other people of being communists or supporting communists. That included your friends and associates, and even then it didn't always work. Witch hunts tend to take on a life of their own. They don't just hurt the people accused. They hurt the people around them and the people who love them, and they hurt the way we all look at our neighbors.

THE DEPRESSION, FASCISM, AND THE SPECIAL COMMITTEE ON UN-AMERICAN ACTIVITIES

From "The Ordeal," an episode of *The Adventures of Robin Hood*, a TV series from the 1950s, written by blacklisted writer Ring Lardner Jr.:

NOBLEMAN: The serfs are getting out of hand.

COUNT: They are beginning to grumble about their food and furnishings. They want beds to sleep on—beds, mind you! Just like us! And two meals a day!

FLY ON THE WALL: During the worldwide Great Depression of the 1930s, many could not fight for themselves. In the United States, one in four people lost their jobs. It looked like the world system was breaking down. Communism's promise to create a better world where workers could be taken care of began to seem tempting to many.

SHEILA SAMPTON: My father was somebody who was fascinated by ideas—definitely an armchair person—and he

loved sharing ideas with his students, and he loved telling stories. I believe that my father's activist days were in the thirties and that one of the reasons to be in the Communist Party was social. It was like a way to meet girls.

ROBIN HOOD: We're never alone as long as we have friends among the people.

JOSH: My father started in the 1930s in the Youth Communist League—and he told me of the pride he felt standing guard outside tenement buildings after the marshal had moved people's furniture out to the street during the Depression. His father and other young communists moved the furniture back in and stood guard outside the buildings, protecting their friends who had lost their jobs and their homes.

J. ROBERT OPPENHEIMER, PHYSICIST: I saw what the Depression was doing to my students . . . I began to understand that deeply political and economic events could affect . . . lives. I began to feel the need to participate more fully in the life of the community.

FLY ON THE WALL: Even though the Depression was worldwide, the reactions weren't the same in every country. In the United States, Franklin Delano Roosevelt was elected president with a "New Deal" for Americans. In the Soviet Union, a powerful dictator, Joseph Stalin, consolidated his power. Instead of peasants getting their own land, he forced them onto collective, mechanized farms. Instead of the poor being better off, they starved.

UKRAINIAN PEASANTS: There is no bread . . . We used to feed the world and now we are hungry.

FLY ON THE WALL: Millions of people died of famine in the Soviet Union, and anyone whom Stalin saw as a threat was executed in purges. Stalin did an excellent job of hiding these facts. Stalin believed in the big lie, and he knew how to sell it.

STALIN: Living has become better, comrades, living has become happier.

FLY ON THE WALL: But in Germany, the response was very different. A new party led by Adolf Hitler rose to power by telling people they were being unfairly treated by a world that did not recognize the superiority of the German race. Hitler was a fascist, and fascists believe that they have a way to save the world. Fascists believe in strong dictators and capitalism and that the power of capitalists and the military are the dominant forces that should run a country. In the United States people were as worried about the rising power of fascists as about the rising power of communists. To protect the country in 1938, the U.S. House of Representatives created the Special Committee on Un-American Activities to hunt down both fascists and communists within the United States, which Congress made permanent in 1945.

COMMITTEE CHAIR MARTIN DIES, DEMOCRAT FROM TEXAS (AUGUST 12, 1938): This committee is determined to conduct its investigation upon a dignified plane and to adopt and maintain a judicial attitude . . . We shall be fair and impartial at all times.

FLY ON THE WALL: They seemed to think that it would be easy to tell what was American and what was not.

DESTROYER OF WORLDS

FLY ON THE WALL: World War II
began in 1939, when Hitler invaded Poland,
and Poland's allies, Britain and France,
declared war on Germany. Most Americans
didn't want to get involved in a "foreign war," but
on December 7, 1941, Hitler's ally Japan bombed
the U.S. Naval Station at Pearl Harbor. The United States declared war
on Japan. Germany and its allies declared war on the United States, and
now it was a war across the globe. Refugees from Nazi-occupied countries fled to the United States, among them many German scientists.

> **DAVID MUNNS, HISTORIAN:** Scientists in Russia, Germany,
> England, and the United States all knew that it was possible to
> unleash unheard-of energy in a nuclear bomb. The question
> was who would do it first.

FLY ON THE WALL: FDR decided the United States had to be the
first to develop the bomb. He authorized the formation of a secret

research team under the leadership of J. Robert Oppenheimer for what was called the Manhattan Project.

Then suddenly, on April 12, 1945 . . .

PRESIDENT ROOSEVELT IS DEAD
LAST WORDS: "I HAVE A TERRIFIC HEADACHE"

FLY ON THE WALL: Roosevelt had been elected to four terms (the only president in American history to do that). Lots of Americans didn't even remember who was vice president. In this case it was Harry S. Truman, a men's clothing salesman-turned-senator from Missouri. Even though nobody, including Roosevelt, had paid attention to Truman (Roosevelt had met one-on-one with his vice president exactly twice), Truman was now the president of the United States.

> **PRESIDENT HARRY S. TRUMAN:** Boys, if you ever pray, pray for me now . . . When they told me yesterday what had happened, I felt like the moon, the stars, and all the planets had fallen on me.

FLY ON THE WALL: One of the things FDR had never gotten around to telling Truman was that he had authorized the creation of an atom bomb. Truman only found out about the Manhattan Project the day after he became president. Three months later, in July 1945, Oppenheimer and his team successfully detonated the world's first atom bomb in the desert of New Mexico.

> **ISIDOR RABI, PHYSICIST:** There was an enormous flash of light, the brightest light I have ever seen or that I think anyone else has ever seen.

TRUMAN (IN HIS DIARY): We have discovered the most terrible bomb in the history of the world.

FLY ON THE WALL: Even though Germany had surrendered on May 7, 1945, the war wasn't over yet. The United States was still fighting Japan, and Americans were dying in the Pacific. Truman asked General George Marshall, the Army chief of staff, how many Americans would likely be killed or wounded in an invasion of Japan. Estimates were at least a quarter million.

TRUMAN: I couldn't worry about what history would say about my personal morality. I made the only decision I ever knew how to make. I did what I thought was right.

FLY ON THE WALL: Truman gave the order to use the atom bomb. On August 6, 1945, the United States dropped the first nuclear bomb on the city of Hiroshima, Japan.

DESTROYER OF WORLDS

COLONEL PAUL TIBBETS, PILOT: We turned back to look at Hiroshima. The city was hidden by that awful cloud . . . boiling up, mushrooming, terrible and incredibly tall.

NAKAMURA IWAO, HIROSHIMA FIFTH GRADER: I had the feeling that all the human beings on the face of the earth had been killed off, and only the five of us were left.

FLY ON THE WALL: Three days later, the United States dropped a second atom bomb, on the Japanese city of Nagasaki.

J. ROBERT OPPENHEIMER, REFLECTING SOBERLY ON WATCHING THE TRINITY TESTS OF THE ATOM BOMB IN NEW MEXICO: We knew the world would not be the same . . . I remembered the line from the Hindu scripture, the Bhagavad Gita . . . "Now I am become death, the destroyer of worlds."

FLY ON THE WALL: Two months later, Oppenheimer went to see Truman in the Oval Office, saying that he felt he had blood on his hands. Truman told aides that he thought Oppenheimer was a crybaby.

TRUMAN: The blood is on my hands. Let me worry about that.

FLY ON THE WALL: Afterward, Truman said he hoped he would not have to see Oppenheimer ever again.

THE AMERICAN DREAM—
WHOOPS, NOT SO FAST

FLY ON THE WALL: Japan surrendered just five days after the atom bomb was dropped on Nagasaki. World War II ended. The United States now stood alone as the most powerful nation in the world. Its only rival was the Soviet Union.

> **OFFICE OF STRATEGIC SERVICES MEMO:** Russia will emerge from the present conflict as by far the strongest nation in Europe and Asia . . . In the easily foreseeable future, Russia may well outrank even the United States in military potential.

FLY ON THE WALL: The threat from the Soviet Union was real. After Germany surrendered, Stalin turned the Allied victory into his personal triumph as he gobbled up all of Eastern Europe.

In March 1946, Winston Churchill, who had been the British prime minister during World War II, traveled to Fulton, Missouri, with Truman at his side and declared:

WINSTON CHURCHILL: From Stettin in the Baltic to Trieste in the Adriatic, an "iron curtain" has descended across the Continent. Behind that line lie all the capitals of the ancient states of Central and Eastern Europe. Warsaw, Berlin, Prague, Vienna, Budapest, Belgrade, Bucharest and Sofia; all these famous cities and the populations around them lie in what I must call the Soviet sphere, and all are subject, in one form or another, not only to Soviet influence but to a very high and, in many cases, increasing measure of control from Moscow.

FLY ON THE WALL: Of course it wasn't literally an iron curtain. Churchill meant that people in the countries that the Soviet Union had taken over were silenced. They were forced to become communists whether they wanted to or not.

A lot of people consider this the official beginning of the Cold War. They called it a cold war because at least in theory no shooting was involved.

LIBRARY OF CONGRESS: Flushed with their success against Germany and Japan in 1945, most Americans initially viewed their place in the postwar world with optimism and confidence.

FLY ON THE WALL: Most Americans were sick of war, hot or cold. After the end of World War II, the United States economy boomed. Americans had saved their money during the war—because there was nothing to buy. Now, all those factories that had been making weapons and uniforms started making cars and clothes and toys . . . and houses. The ultimate American dream was to own your own house. In communist countries, nobody could own anything, especially a house.

> **WILLIAM LEVITT, DEVELOPER:** No man who owns his own house and lot can be a communist.

FLY ON THE WALL: The problem was, not all Americans could own a house—even if they had money to pay for it.

> **LEVITTOWN STANDARD LEASE (1948):** Premises [cannot] be used or occupied by any person other than members of the Caucasian race.

FLY ON THE WALL: Levitt said it was just a business decision. White buyers would not want to buy a house if they thought that they would have Black neighbors.

> **WILLIAM LEVITT:** The plain fact is that most whites prefer not to live in mixed communities. This attitude may be wrong morally, and someday it may change. I hope it will.

FLY ON THE WALL: Of course, often Jews were not allowed to buy houses, and sometimes Catholics too had been kept out.

EUGENE BURNETT, BLACK WAR VETERAN: [I still sting from] the feeling of rejection on that long ride back to Harlem.

HARRY BELAFONTE, BLACK ENTERTAINER: I came out of the service with great expectations that we had just defeated fascism. We'd just defeated totalitarianism. We had just defeated the philosophy of white supremacy. . . . I had expected America would have been open and generous and rewarding to its Black citizens who had served in the war, and served with great honor.

WADE HUDSON, WRITER: My father had risked his life for democracy, but, for him, freedom remained just a stale hope, a wishful thought, an unfulfilled dream.

FLY ON THE WALL: For some returning Black veterans, being denied home ownership was the least of their concerns. Isaac Woodard, a twenty-six-year-old Black sergeant, was discharged with $744.73 of pay from the Army, which was a lot of money in those days. On February 12, 1946 (Lincoln's birthday), Woodard got on a bus in Augusta, Georgia, to reunite with his wife in South Carolina. A lot of other discharged soldiers were on the bus celebrating together. Some civilians complained to the driver about the whites and Blacks mingling. About an hour into the ride, Woodard asked the driver to wait a little longer for him at a scheduled stop. There were no toilets in buses then.

ALTON BLACKWELL, BUS DRIVER: Hell, no. God damn it, go back and sit down. I ain't got time to wait.

WOODARD: God damn it, talk to me like I am talking to you. I am a man just like you.

FLY ON THE WALL: At the next stop the driver got off the bus and went to get the police.

BLACKWELL: This soldier has been making a disturbance on the bus.

FLY ON THE WALL: A police officer told Woodard to shut up and get off the bus.

WOODARD: He asked me was I discharged . . . When I said, "yes," that is when he started beating me with the billy, hitting me across the top of my head . . . When we got to the door of the police station, he struck me again and knocked me unconscious. After I commenced to come to myself, he hollered, "Get up." When I started to get up, he started punching me in my eyes with the end of his billy.

FLY ON THE WALL: As a result of the beating, Woodard was blinded.

ROBERT YOUNG, WOODARD'S NEPHEW: He told me they poured whiskey over him to say he was drunk. He was arrested for, supposedly, disorderly conduct, disturbing the peace and being drunk. He was not drunk. He was not being disorderly. And he did not disturb the peace.

TIME: Woodard's blinding was . . . a political awakening for future civil rights leaders. Student Nonviolent Coordinating Committee co-founder Julian Bond's earliest memory of racial violence was seeing newspaper photographs of Woodard with bandages over his eyes at the age of six.

WASHINGTON POST: Hundreds of Black veterans had been attacked and an unknown number were lynched . . . One Black veteran had been murdered for casting a vote in a primary.

FLY ON THE WALL: In July 1946, four Black people, including a medaled veteran and his wife, were beaten, tortured, shot, and hanged from a bridge in Georgia. It is considered the last mass lynching in America.

CIVIL RIGHTS, TRUMAN, AND
ENTER TAIL GUNNER JOE

TIM WEINER, HISTORIAN: The FBI had spied on every prominent black political figure in America since World War I . . . Hoover spent his career convinced that communism was behind the civil rights movement in the United States from the start.

FLY ON THE WALL: With returning veterans trying to assert their rights, Hoover felt it was his duty to warn Truman and Congress that anyone who was fighting for Black rights was falling for the communist line. The NAACP *had* been looking for test cases to show the American people how Black veterans who had fought in the war were being treated. Woodard, polite and handsome, walked into the NAACP offices and told his story in a sworn affidavit.

KENNETH MACK, HISTORIAN: The NAACP leadership was always on the lookout for cases of injustice that they could use to really dramatize the nature of the Southern racial system.

FLY ON THE WALL: The NAACP sent Woodard on a speaking tour and held a fundraiser for him. Civil rights leaders hoped that the outrage about Woodard's story would help their movement to desegregate the Army.

> **WOODARD:** I spent three and a half years in service to my country and thought that I would be treated like a man when I returned to civilian life, but I was mistaken.

> **A. PHILIP RANDOLPH, CIVIL RIGHTS LEADER:** The matter of discrimination and segregation in the armed forces . . . is a grave threat to Negro youth and to the internal stability of our nation. Segregation becomes all the more important at a time when the United States should be assuming moral leadership in the world.

FLY ON THE WALL: Truman had grown up in the segregated south. He also understood how important segregation and white supremacy were to the Democratic Party. Truman was reluctant at first to put his shaky political capital on the line. He told his appointments secretary to tell the NAACP that it wasn't possible for the President to meet with them. But A. Philip Randolph and his chief lieutenant Bayard Rustin were not ready to accept "not possible" as an answer. Instead they organized a picket of the White House.

> **BAYARD RUSTIN, CIVIL RIGHTS ACTIVIST:** If we must die for our country, let us die as free men—not as Jim Crow slaves.

FLY ON THE WALL: Truman was a veteran himself, and the stories of Isaac Woodard and other returning veterans had really shaken him.

TRUMAN: When a Mayor and City Marshal can take a negro Sergeant off a bus in South Carolina, beat him up and put out one of his eyes, and nothing is done about it by the State Authorities, something is radically wrong with the system.

FLY ON THE WALL: On December 5, 1946, Truman issued an executive order he called "Freedom from Fear," which created the first President's Committee on Civil Rights.

TRUMAN: My forebears were confederates . . . But my very stomach turned over when I learned that Negro soldiers, just back from overseas, were being dumped out of army trucks in Mississippi and beaten.

Whatever my inclinations as a native of Missouri might have been, as President I know this is bad. I shall fight to end evils like this.

FLY ON THE WALL: Truman presented Congress with his ideas for a civil rights commission and federal legislation against lynching and poll taxes. By 1946, Republicans hadn't been in control of Congress for fifteen years. They were hungry. Truman wasn't nearly as popular as FDR had been. And they used his civil rights stance to hint that he was secretly a communist sympathizer. They called him soft on communism.

REPUBLICAN SLOGAN, 1946: Had Enough! To Err is Truman.

FLY ON THE WALL: Calling Truman soft on Communism was a successful Republican rallying cry. In the 1946 midterm elections, the Republicans gained control of both houses of Congress for the first time in sixteen years. The newly elected "class of 1946" had two future presidents, John F. Kennedy and Richard Nixon, but they weren't the ones getting the headlines. Those went to a little-known Republican junior senator from Wisconsin, Joseph McCarthy. In his Senate campaign, McCarthy called himself Tail Gunner Joe and bragged about his military heroics even though he had never actually been a tail gunner. The first thing he did upon arriving in Washington was to call a news conference.

REPORTER: What makes you think you're important enough to call a press conference?

FLY ON THE WALL: McCarthy just changed the subject. The press loved him.

SATURDAY EVENING POST: He is a muscular six-footer, with long arms and square, capable hands, and his physical movements are the quick purposeful ones of the good athlete . . . McCarthy is pleased by his occasional anonymity and works hard at being informal and approachable. He encourages the guards and elevator operators in the Senate Office Building to call him "Joe," and they do . . . To woo the women correspondents, he invited eight from the Senate press gallery to a fried-chicken dinner. . . . McCarthy cooked the dinner himself.

TEACHERS, BEWARE

FLY ON THE WALL: Republicans had started a brush fire, heating up a fear of communism, and it spread. Local governments and school boards soon took up the hunt for hidden communists in their midst. One easy target was teachers. After all, teachers usually spent more time with kids than their parents did. And a lot of times, kids believed their teachers. A teacher could spread communism just like the flu. State and local governments formed their own committees to investigate subversive activities.

CLARENCE TAYLOR, AUTHOR OF *REDS AT THE BLACKBOARD*: Teachers saw children coming to school hungry—and the teachers union tried to make sure they had adequate food. You had dedicated teachers on behalf of students—and then one day they are taken out of the classroom—they disappear.

FRANCES EISENBERG, CALIFORNIA TEACHER: The teaching profession as a whole was frightened into submissiveness. At one point a bunch of us had written to Albert Einstein and said, "What shall we do?"

EINSTEIN, ACCORDING TO EISENBERG: Become plumbers, become anything, but do not sign the loyalty oath.

JAMES BALDWIN, ACCORDING TO HISTORIAN CLARENCE TAYLOR: It was a shame that teachers, who cared about their Black students in Harlem, were banned from the classroom.

FLY ON THE WALL: Some teachers did try to defend themselves. Anne Hale was a second-grade teacher in Massachusetts who had once been a member of the Communist Party but had lost interest and stopped paying her dues. FBI agents warned school officials that there was a subversive in their midst. The Wayland School Committee called Anne Hale in for a private meeting. She read a three-page statement.

HALE: My six years as a teacher . . . have been the happiest and more rewarding years of my life so far. [The Pledge of Allegiance] is no idle pledge for me.

COMMITTEE MEMBERS CORNELIUS MAGUIRE AND HARVEY NEWTON: The mind of a child is particularly receptive. It is important for children, even in the lower grades, to be taught by teachers imbued with our American ideas of democracy, loyalty, love of country and respect for our tradition of freedom.

FLY ON THE WALL: Hale was suspended without pay. After a hearing that lasted three weeks, she was fired. Out of a job and out of money, she took a night job cleaning dog kennels. The FBI confirmed to her new boss that there was a subversive on his staff, and she was fired again.

WAYLAND TOWN CRIER EDITORIAL: Rumor and gossip have had a field day. Excited by the discovery of a former

Communist in town, [citizens] have jumped to the conclusion that there must be others.

FLY ON THE WALL: All over the country, anything could make people suspicious that there were communists among them. Here are some real-life examples:

- His dog had a red leash.
- A blinking porch light could be a signal.
- A pitcher contained red Kool-Aid.
- On a laundry line hung red shirts and pants.
- Red window shutters might be relaying coded Soviet messages.

ARE COMMUNISTS HIDING IN HOLLYWOOD?

FLY ON THE WALL: Republicans were excited. They finally had control of Congress—all of it. And they had an enforcer—the House Un-American Activities Committee. All they needed now was a headline. What better place to look for one than at the movies?

FBI ASSOCIATE DIRECTOR CLYDE TOLSON (TO HOOVER): [HUAC was] interested in finding out what we were doing with respect to the Communist picture in the movie industry.

FLY ON THE WALL: Hoover and the FBI were happy to cooperate. The committee scheduled public hearings on communists in Hollywood for October 1947. The hearings opened in Washington, D.C., with all the glitz the movie industry was famous for. They even had a camera check and found that HUAC Chair J. Parnell Thomas was so short that he needed a boost to be seen properly by the cameras. They had to put a phone book on his chair, and when that wasn't enough, they added a pillow. Klieg lights replaced the ornate crystal chandeliers. Four radio networks would be broadcasting gavel to gavel.

> **HOLLYWOOD REPORTER (OCTOBER 20, 1947):**
> Despite . . . being Washington's largest hearing room, space for the public [would] be SRO [standing room only].

FLY ON THE WALL: Walt Disney was a name everybody knew. He was much beloved, and he hated communists and unions.

> **WALT DISNEY, MOVIE PRODUCER:** The thing that I resent the most is that [communists] are able to get into these unions, [and] take them over . . . I feel that they really ought to be smoked out and shown up for what they are, so that all of the good, free causes in this country, all the liberalisms that really are American, can go out without the taint of communism. That is my sincere feeling on it.

> **H. A. SMITH, COMMITTEE INVESTIGATOR:** Do you feel that there is a threat of communism in the motion-picture industry?

> **DISNEY:** Yes, there is, and there are many reasons . . . but I don't think they have gotten very far, and I think the industry is made up of good Americans.

FLY ON THE WALL: Then the committee got to work on the juicy parts. First up the next week was John Howard Lawson, the president of the Screen Writers' Guild, who had been a communist in the late 1930s and never hid it.

LAWSON: Mr. Chairman, I have a statement here which I wish to make.

FLY ON THE WALL: The statement was handed to the Chairman, who looked at it, read the first line silently, and glared.

CHAIR PARNELL THOMAS, REPUBLICAN FROM NEW JERSEY: The statement will not be read. I read the first line.

FLY ON THE WALL: The beginning of the statement read, "For a week, this Committee has conducted an illegal and indecent trial of American citizens, whom the Committee has selected to be publicly pilloried and smeared." *Pilloried* means put in the stocks—the kind where your head sticks out and people throw vegetables at you.

LAWSON: I am being treated differently from the rest.

FLY ON THE WALL: And, of course, he was. They never cut off Walt Disney.

THOMAS: Mr. Lawson, you will have to stop or you will leave the witness stand. And you will leave the witness stand because you are in contempt.

LAWSON: I am glad you have made it perfectly clear that you are going to threaten and intimidate the witnesses.

FLY ON THE WALL: The committee chair pounded his gavel as loudly as he could. But Lawson was in show business; he knew how to talk over a gavel.

LAWSON: I am an American and I am not at all easy to intimidate.

FLY ON THE WALL: The committee grilled him about his position in the Screen Writers' Guild, then finally got to the question they wanted to ask.

ROBERT E. STRIPLING, COMMITTEE INVESTIGATOR: Are you now, or have you ever been, a member of the Communist Party of the United States?

FLY ON THE WALL: Here it was. The big question that the Red Scare witch hunts would be famous for.

THOMAS: Now, do you care to answer that question?

LAWSON: You are using the old technique, which was used in Hitler Germany, in order to create a scare here.

FLY ON THE WALL: The chairman pounded his gavel some more.

LAWSON: The Bill of Rights was established precisely to prevent the operation of any committee which could invade the basic rights of Americans.

FLY ON THE WALL: Actually, he was right.

FIRST AMENDMENT OF THE CONSTITUTION: Congress shall make no law . . . abridging the freedom of speech, or of the press; or the right of people peaceably to assemble, and to petition the Government for a redress of grievances.

FLY ON THE WALL: The committee chair pounded away desperately.

LAWSON: It is unfortunate and tragic that I have to teach this committee the basic principles of American—

THOMAS (RAISING HIS VOICE): That is not the question. That is not the question. The question is: Have you ever been a member of the Communist Party?

LAWSON: I have told you that I will offer my beliefs, affiliations, and everything else to the American public.

THOMAS: Excuse the witness. [Pounds gavel.] Stand away from the stand—

LAWSON (RAISING HIS VOICE): I shall continue to fight for the Bill of Rights, which you are trying to destroy.

THOMAS: Officers, take this man away from the stand.

FLY ON THE WALL: Even after Lawson was forced to leave the hearing, the committee continued hauling writers onto the stand, which actually was a really bad idea because many writers like to talk—and can often be quite funny. One was the writer Dalton Trumbo, a man who liked to write in the bathtub while smoking a cigar.

INVESTIGATOR STRIPLING (TO TRUMBO): I shall ask various questions, all of which can be answered "Yes" or "No."

TRUMBO: Very many questions can be answered "Yes" or "No" only by a moron or a slave.

FLY ON THE WALL: They called the writer Ring Lardner Jr. Unfortunately for them, he was just as funny and clever as Trumbo.

> **THOMAS:** It's a very simple question. . . . Any real American would be proud to answer the question, "Are you or have you ever been a member of the Communist Party?"

> **LARDNER:** I could answer it, but if I did, I would hate myself in the morning.

FLY ON THE WALL: HUAC was beginning to catch on that it was a bad idea to give center stage to writers who were more clever than the committee ever could be. Committee chair Thomas ended the Hollywood hearings. Lawson, Trumbo, Lardner, and seven others were indicted for contempt of Congress. They would be convicted the next year and sent to jail when the U.S. Supreme Court upheld their convictions.

TRUMBO: As far as I was concerned, it was a completely just verdict. I had contempt for that Congress, and I've had contempt for several since.

RED LIST, GRAY LIST, EVERYBODY'S GOT A LIST

CINEMA EDUCATIONAL GUILD PAMPHLET:
AMERICANS: DON'T PATRONIZE REDS! YOU CAN
DRIVE THE REDS OUT OF TELEVISION, RADIO
AND HOLLYWOOD . . . RIGHT NOW films are being
made to craftily glorify MARXISM, UNESCO and
ONE-WORLDISM . . . and via your TV Set, they are being
piped into your Living Room—and are poisoning the minds
of your children under your very eyes!

TRUMAN: People are very much wrought up about the
Communist bugaboo, but I am of the opinion that the country
is perfectly safe as far as Communism is concerned—we have
too many sane people.

FLY ON THE WALL: But the Hollywood trials had everyone convinced that communists were hiding everywhere. As in 1946, Republicans were effectively using a fear of communists as a tool against

Truman when he ran for election. Truman *wanted* to run for president in 1948, and he knew the only way to do it was to prove he could be as anticommunist as anybody else. In 1947, Truman launched the Federal Employees Loyalty Program.

> **CLARK CLIFFORD, TRUMAN'S POLITICAL STRATEGIST:**
> The Republicans have tried to identify the Administration with the domestic Communists. The President adroitly stole their thunder.

FLY ON THE WALL: On the other hand, Truman didn't want to go too far. He knew the danger of witch hunts. After all, he believed that plenty of people who worked for the government were loyal.

> **TRUMAN:** I believe I speak for all the people of the United States when I say that subversive elements must be removed from the employ of the Government . . . The overwhelming majority of Federal employees are loyal citizens . . . do not want them to fear they are the objects of any "witch hunt."

FLY ON THE WALL: Truman was fooling himself. He fooled himself into thinking that he could hunt communists in the government and at the same time protect American liberties. Others in government who were fighting to increase their own power found hunting communists very effective—perhaps no one more than J. Edgar Hoover.

Hoover, who had started out as a messenger for the Library of Congress, collected what would become an infamous and somewhat secret list of thousands of names, mostly U.S. citizens, whom he suspected were communist sympathizers. Hoover and the Justice Department published the list with the catchy name: the Attorney General's List of Subversive Organizations (AGLOSO).

TIMES-HERALD (WASHINGTON, D.C.): Here is a round dozen of the better known of these gangs which the U.S. Department of Justice has officially labeled subversive: National Negro Congress, Protestant War Veterans of the United States, Inc., Washington Bookshop Association.

FLY ON THE WALL: And Hoover had more than one tool to use against what he saw as threats. The Smith Act of 1940 made it illegal to advocate or teach the overthrow of the government or to belong to a group advocating or taking such action. It passed the House of Representatives 382–4, but it wasn't used during World War II because the Soviet Union was our ally. But on January 27, 1948, Hoover wanted to use the Smith Act to indict people in the Communist Party.

HOOVER: Once the precedent is set, the members and adherents can be dealt with as violators.

FLY ON THE WALL: Hoover's dry language can make you forget that the people who had joined the Communist Party when it was legal were real; they had families and friends and lives.

JOSH, SON OF A COMMUNIST PARTY MEMBER: My father was a paid organizer for the American Communist Party for twenty-five years. Suddenly he had to go underground and live under an assumed name in Buffalo, New York. One day— another comrade showed up at the door and said to my mother:

COMRADE: Pack up Josh, we're leaving today. We're driving up to Buffalo.

JOSH: She had probably been away from my father for about four months.

MOTHER: I'm not leaving today—because I have not packed up Josh's toys.

COMRADE: Oh come on, you can buy other toys when we get where we're going.

MOTHER: Yeah, but they won't be HIS toys. They won't be Josh's toys.

JOSH: That story always meant a lot to me. That my mother thought I was more important than politics.

FLY ON THE WALL: Soon you even had to sign a loyalty oath to get a fishing license. You couldn't be a preschool teacher or a librarian without signing a loyalty oath.

GRIFFIN FARIELLO, HISTORIAN: Neighbors informed on neighbors, students on their teachers. Readers of "questionable" works hid their leftist tomes or buried them in the back garden.

FLY ON THE WALL: But some Americans fought back. For example, students in Indiana weren't going to take an attack on Robin Hood lying down.

LOUISE DERMAN-SPARKS, TEACHER WHO WAS A HIGH SCHOOL STUDENT IN THE 1950S: When Robin Hood (who I had always loved) was attacked—that was the last straw.

FLY ON THE WALL: In the spirit of patriotism, five enterprising Indiana University students made a quick trip to a local poultry farm and stuffed six burlap sacks with feathers—easy to do because feathers don't weigh much. They dyed the feathers green in honor of the feather Robin Hood wore in his hat. Then they tossed them around the university campus to protest censorship. The FBI showed up to investigate.

ADA WHITE, MEMBER OF INDIANA TEXTBOOK COMMISSION: There is a Communist directive in education now to stress the story of Robin Hood. They want to stress it because he robbed the rich and gave it to the poor. That's the Communist line. It's just a smearing of law and order and anything that disrupts law and order is their meat.

J. EDGAR HOOVER: The best antidote to communism is vigorous, intelligent, old-fashioned Americanism with eternal vigilance.

FLY ON THE WALL: But the United States wasn't founded on eternal vigilance. It was founded on a people's right and obligation to question their government.

DECLARATION OF INDEPENDENCE: Whenever any form of government becomes destructive of these ends [life, liberty,

and the pursuit of happiness], it is the right of the people to alter or to abolish it.

FLY ON THE WALL: When the FBI showed up, the students got scared. They worried they'd be kicked out of school or wind up in jail.

HOOVER: Communists . . . can teach our youth a way of life that eventually will destroy the sanctity of the home, that undermines faith in God, that causes them to scorn respect for constituted authority and sabotage our revered Constitution.

GEORGE WASHINGTON: Freedom of speech may be taken away, and dumb and silent, we may be led, like sheep, to the slaughter.

REAL PEOPLE, REAL FEAR

FLY ON THE WALL: A lot of people worried what to do if their name ended up on one of the lists labeled as subversive.

ELKS MAGAZINE (NOVEMBER 1956): There are few Americans who have not heard of "the Attorney General's subversive list."

FLY ON THE WALL: Some of the questions people had to answer to prove they were loyal were silly, and some were very personal.

QUESTION: There is suspicion in the record that you are in sympathy with the underprivileged. Is this true?

QUESTION: Have you ever had Negroes in your home?

QUESTION: In your recollection, do you recall ever discussing any topic which might be sympathetic to Communist doctrine?

FLY ON THE WALL: Neighbors started turning in neighbors. Soon a lot of people were looking over their shoulders, afraid that anybody at any moment might call them a communist and they'd lose their jobs.

> **PETER FRANK:** My parents left their jobs in television. My mother was one of the first women in television. My parents had been working on *Candid Camera*. They realized with the blacklist they weren't going to be able to continue to work in television. They had both been active communists in the 1930s. My mother had left the party long before the 1950s because she didn't like the way they treated women. We moved to a farm in Connecticut. When the FBI came to visit my parents on the farm, my dad said to me, "Don't worry, communist chickens don't make headlines, and that's what they're looking for."

FLY ON THE WALL: Everyone had a list—*Counterattack*, Aware, HUAC, *Red Channels*, the attorney general, the State Department, J. Edgar Hoover, the Ku Klux Klan. Some of the best people in the business were being blacklisted.

> **JOE GILFORD, SON OF BLACKLISTED ACTOR JACK GILFORD:** We were lucky. No one close to us was an informer. Witch hunters are afraid that if they don't hunt enough, they will also be accused. But what's strange about the blacklist is that they didn't publish a real list—they just let nature and the economy take their course.

FLY ON THE WALL: There were plenty of different lists. One of the most famous was *Red Channels*, with names of people in radio and television.

HARRY BELAFONTE: When I first discovered [I was on] the blacklist I had gone to see my agent . . . He pulled out a drawer in his desk, reached for a phone—it was not part of the regular phone bank. He dialed a number, and all he did was to give my name, Harry Belafonte. And then he waited for instruction, and then he hung up the phone, closed the drawer, and said, "You're on the list. You're unemployable."

FLY ON THE WALL: In 1954, Belafonte won the Tony Award for best featured actor in a musical. By tradition, Tony winners were supposed to appear on *The Ed Sullivan Show*, a popular TV variety show of the 1950s, but Belafonte was considered unacceptable. Sullivan called him into his office and read him a list of things he had been accused of.

BELAFONTE: I said to him that many of the things on the list were true and other things on the list were false . . . That is not really the issue. The issue is my right to privacy, my right to my beliefs as an American citizen, and that I was sorry that I did not have the opportunity to be on his show. I would dearly have loved to do so; it would have meant a lot to my career, and I thanked him and I left. That evening I got a call from the very same agent . . . to tell me that I was on *The Ed Sullivan Show* and that I should be prepared to go to rehearsals that Saturday and Sunday and that I would be on the air live that same weekend. This fact and this act forever took me off the blacklist. But what it did do was that it instantly raised significant suspicion among my colleagues that I had betrayed them, because there was no way for me to have gotten on *The Ed Sullivan Show* if I had not played the betrayal game. And it was a very, very, very difficult time for me.

FLY ON THE WALL: One of the cruelest parts of the Red Scare was that not only were you suspected of being a communist—and labeled a communist—but you were also asked to give names and betray your friends. HUAC made it clear that the only way you could survive was by naming names, and so even if you didn't name names and your career went on, then everyone believed you had turned in your friends.

> **JOE GILFORD:** My parents were proud of never having named names. Anyone who named, they were finks. They were rats who did it only to save themselves. My parents did not believe those people were doing it to be patriotic.

> **OSSIE DAVIS, BLACK ACTOR:** We figured we would go crazy if we tried to figure out whether we were blacklisted because we were Black or blacklisted because we were Red.

FLY ON THE WALL: Writers—even the ones who went to jail—had an easier time than actors. In the 1940s, Paul Robeson was one of the most famous Black American entertainers.

> **MARTIN DUBERMAN, HISTORIAN:** White Americans praised him as proof that "the system" worked.

FLY ON THE WALL: Robeson traveled the world as a singer and, in 1934, had gone to Moscow, where he was greeted as a hero. In late August 1949, Robeson was planning to give a concert in a park near Peekskill, New York. When his fans came to hear him, they were met by people with baseball bats, who blocked their cars and buses and jeered, "Dirty commies." Crosses were burned on a hill overlooking the concert venue.

TOBY EMMER: My father was on honor guard to try to protect Paul Robeson . . . Our bus was hit with rocks—my mother covered us with sweaters. My brother was with me. I think he was five. Later when he had to take the school bus to kindergarten, he was scared.

TOBY EMMER'S BROTHER: I'm not going on the bus . . . the bad boys throw stones.

FLY ON THE WALL: Paul Robeson's career never recovered. Entertainers were especially vulnerable to being blacklisted. They needed audiences.

RING LARDNER JR.: By the time we came out of prison in 1951, the whole situation had gotten worse. Senator McCarthy had come onto the scene in the meantime . . . Then it really clamped down in Hollywood. . . .

I also wrote for television on the blacklist. It was my main source of income during the fifties . . . [I] wrote pilot films for television shows shot in England. The first one we did was called *The Adventures of Robin Hood*. That survived on American television for three or four years; it was quite a popular show.

FLY ON THE WALL: Pretty ironic because of the controversy over Robin Hood robbing from the rich and giving to the poor!

EDGAR, ONE OF ROBIN'S OUTLAWS: [Robin Hood is] a man who'll be remembered when these cruel lords and fat sheriffs will long be forgotten.

THE BERLIN AIRLIFT AND THE
START OF POLITICS ON TV

FLY ON THE WALL: An amazing thing happened in 1948. For the first time, presidential conventions were going to be broadcast live from Philadelphia in the middle of the summer.

> **JACK GOULD, *NEW YORK TIMES* REPORTER:** Television adds to the interest of the exciting convention.

FLY ON THE WALL: On June 24, 1948, on the very day that Republican candidate Thomas E. Dewey accepted his nomination live on prime-time television, the Soviet Union announced it was cutting off all ground access to the western sectors of Berlin. After World War II, the victors—the United States, France, Britain, and the Soviet Union—were each given a sector. Berlin, the capital of Germany, was in the Soviet sector. But the city itself was also split into four sectors, which is how the United States, France, and Britain had a foothold in the middle of Soviet territory. Many people worried that Stalin's communist blockade might lead to World War III. While some felt that the United States should take aggressive action, Truman had other ideas. He ordered the U.S. Air Force to supply Berlin, which just a few years earlier the United States had bombed into rubble.

GAIL HALVORSEN, PILOT: I'll never forget my first flight to Berlin. From the air the city looked like a moonscape. How could 2 million people live in a place like this? I couldn't wait to deliver the 20,000 pounds of flour we had onboard. Berlin needed food and freedom. We had both.

FLY ON THE WALL: The airlift, along with supplies and food, even parachuted candy in for the children.

CHRISTA SCHNEIDER, WHO WAS A CHILD IN BERLIN: You kept us alive.

FLY ON THE WALL: Actually, it wasn't just candy that kept them alive, but the coal, food, and medicine. The airlift made Truman a hero in Berlin, but Americans were tired of worrying about Germany, and the airlift didn't improve his popularity by much at first. As Truman got ready to go to the Democratic Convention in Philadelphia, his poll numbers were in the toilet, down to 38 percent.

NEWSWEEK: Only a miracle or a series of political blunders not to be expected of a man of Dewey's astuteness can save Truman.

CLARE BOOTHE LUCE, REPUBLICAN POLITICIAN: Frankly, he's a gone goose.

FLY ON THE WALL: It was even hotter than it had been two weeks earlier when the Republicans met in the same convention hall.

SENATOR ALBEN BARKLEY, DEMOCRAT FROM KENTUCKY: You could cut the gloom with a corn knife. The very air smelled of defeat.

FLY ON THE WALL: Of course, not everybody was doom and gloom. There were plenty of people who were excited.

HAL ROSENTHAL: I was 17 years old, tried to sneak into the convention and failed. So I went to a local bar to watch on the small, round, black and white TV set.

FLY ON THE WALL: A woman asked Rosenthal what he was doing there, and he told her he wanted to go to the Democratic Convention but couldn't get in.

> **WOMAN:** It is hot, sweaty, and crowded, but I'll lend you my credentials.

FLY ON THE WALL: This is sort of like a backstage pass, kind of like being with the band. Each delegate gets one, and she was a delegate from Minnesota.

> **ROSENTHAL:** So there I was, having never ventured past the Schuylkill River [in Philadelphia], now an alternate delegate from Minnesota.

FLY ON THE WALL: The Minnesota delegation was led by the mayor of Minneapolis, Hubert Humphrey, who spoke on the convention floor on the final day and urged delegates to adopt Truman's civil rights program as a plank in the party platform.

> **HUMPHREY:** To those who say we are rushing this issue of civil rights—I say to them we are 172 years late! . . . The time has arrived in America for the Democratic Party to get out of the shadows of states' rights and walk forthrightly into the bright sunshine of human rights.

FLY ON THE WALL: The civil rights platform passed. Delegations from the Southern states were furious. As the states' roll call to nominate the party's presidential candidate began, half the southerners who remained promptly nominated their own last-minute candidate rather than support Truman and his civil rights plan.

CHARLES J. BLOCH, DELEGATE FROM MACON, GEORGIA: You shall not crucify the South on this cross of civil rights.

FLY ON THE WALL: With all the speechmaking during the states' roll call, it wasn't until 12:42 a.m. that Truman won the nomination, nearly two in the morning before he actually spoke. Just before he was introduced, forty-eight white pigeons, one for each state, representing "doves of peace," were released. Unfortunately, the birds had been

cooped up in the heat, and they frantically flew every which way. Truman said one landed on the bald head of convention Chairman Sam Rayburn of Texas.

RAYBURN: Harry Truman's a goddamn liar. No pigeon ever lit on my head.

COMMUNIST SPIES AND TRUMAN LOSES (OR DOES HE?)

FLY ON THE WALL: Two days after the Democratic convention, the "Dixiecrats," the Southern Democrats who supported states' rights, got together in Alabama and nominated their own candidate for president, Strom Thurmond, the governor of South Carolina.

> **THURMOND:** We have been stabbed in the back by a president who has betrayed every principle of the Democratic Party in his desire to win at any cost.

FLY ON THE WALL: While the Democrats were destroying each other over civil rights, the Republicans had a winning issue: Communism—it was a sure crowd-pleaser. Ambitious Republicans in Congress wanted to make it their own.

> **REPRESENTATIVE SAM RAYBURN, DEMOCRAT FROM TEXAS:** There is political dynamite in this Communist investigation. Don't doubt that.

FLY ON THE WALL: In the heat of that same summer, Whittaker Chambers, a senior editor at *Time* magazine, testified before the House Un-American Activities Committee. He claimed that he had been an important figure in the American Communist Party in the 1930s but was now a "patriot."

> **CHAMBERS (TESTIFYING BEFORE HUAC):** For a number of years I had myself served in the underground, chiefly in Washington, D.C . . . I knew it at its top level . . . A member of this group . . . was Alger Hiss.

FLY ON THE WALL: Alger Hiss was the golden boy of the State Department. He came from an old, distinguished family. Whittaker Chambers was a pudgy, disheveled man. Hiss was tall, slim, and quite elegant. Alger Hiss took the stand two days later.

> **HISS:** I am here at my own request to deny unqualifiedly various statements about me which were made before this committee by one Whittaker Chambers . . . I am not and never have been a member of the Communist Party . . . I have never followed the Communist Party line, directly or indirectly.

FLY ON THE WALL: The Republican Party was thrilled with headlines about spies in Truman's State Department.

> **REPORTER:** Mr. President, do you think that the Capitol Hill spy scare is a "red herring"?

TRUMAN: Yes, I do . . . The public hearings now under way are serving no useful purpose. On the contrary, they are doing irreparable harm to certain people, seriously impairing the morale of federal employees, and undermining public confidence in the government. And they are simply a "red herring" to keep from doing what they ought to do.

FLY ON THE WALL: J. Edgar Hoover had thrown his weight behind the Republicans, and Republican presidential candidate Thomas E. Dewey had promised Hoover he would name him as his attorney general.

WILLIAM SULLIVAN, HOOVER ASSISTANT: The FBI helped Dewey during the campaign itself by giving him everything we had that could hurt Truman, though there wasn't much.

FLY ON THE WALL: Dewey played the communist card for all it was worth.

DEWEY: Communists and fellow travelers [have] risen to positions of trust in our government . . . [and yet] the head of our own government called the exposure of Communists in our government "a red herring."

FLY ON THE WALL: As the campaign heated up in the fall of 1948, nobody believed that Truman could win.

NEWSWEEK: The landslide for Dewey will sweep the country.

LOS ANGELES TIMES: Mr. Truman is the most complete

fumbler and blunderer this nation has seen in high office in a long time.

FLY ON THE WALL: Meanwhile, Truman used the old-fashioned, crowd-pleasing campaign technique of crisscrossing the country on a train and stopping at every town to give a speech from the caboose. The crowds greeting him kept getting bigger and more enthusiastic.

DEMOCRAT SAM RAYBURN, HOUSE MINORITY LEADER: He is good on the back of a train because he is one of the folks. He smiles with them and not at them, laughs with them and not at them.

FLY ON THE WALL: But Dewey's numbers in the polls stayed firmly ahead. In Gallup's last poll before the election, he was up by five points. The night of November 3, 1948, the *Chicago Tribune* prematurely published a gigantic headline.

CHICAGO TRIBUNE: DEWEY DEFEATS TRUMAN

FLY ON THE WALL: Late on election night, it turned out the Gallup poll numbers were exactly right. They were just backward. Truman beat Dewey by five points. The day after the election, Truman was photographed holding up the early edition of the *Chicago Tribune* newspaper.

THE PERFECT MAN
TO LIGHT THE FIRE

FLY ON THE WALL: The end of World War II had left China in a civil war as communists led by Mao Tse-tung and nationalists led by Chiang Kai-shek fought for control of the country after the occupying Japanese forces withdrew. After four years of fighting, Mao took control, and on October 1, 1949, China became a communist country.

SAM RUSHAY, ARCHIVIST AT TRUMAN LIBRARY: President Truman was blamed for the communist victory in China.

FLY ON THE WALL: In advance of the midterm elections of 1950, the Republicans saw a way to use the growing fear that an international communist revolution would sweep the world and drown American democracy and freedom in its wake.

REPUBLICAN STATEMENT OF PRINCIPLES AND OBJECTIVES: We deplore the dangerous degree to which

Communists and their fellow travelers have been employed in important Government posts . . . We denounce the soft attitude of this Administration toward Government employees and officials who hold or support Communist attitudes.

FLY ON THE WALL: Republicans had a game plan. They would fan out across the country and play up the communist threat. Republican politicians competed for the best speaking spots—Chicago, St. Louis, San Francisco—not a dinner put on by the Ohio County Republican Women's Club in Wheeling, West Virginia. But that's where they sent freshman Senator Joe McCarthy. Not exactly a plum assignment. Only the local paper and radio station showed up to cover it. The ladies were happy to see him. McCarthy always did well with female voters. Little did they know that they would hear one of the most notorious speeches in American history.

McCARTHY: I have here in my hand a list of 205—a list of names that were made known to the Secretary of State as being members of the Communist Party and who nevertheless are still working and shaping policy in the State Department.

FLY ON THE WALL: Republicans were always saying that communists riddled the State Department, but they were usually careful not to use specific numbers.

EDITOR OF THE *WHEELING INTELLIGENCER*:
Did McCarthy really give a specific number?

FRANK DESMOND, *WHEELING INTELLIGENCER* REPORTER: Joe said it was 205.

FLY ON THE WALL: When reporter Frank Desmond went to listen to the tape again, he found out the tape had been erased a day or two after it was broadcast. It wasn't a conspiracy—that's what the station always did with tapes. That's the thing about the historical record—it has holes. But McCarthy had put out a specific number, and this was big news. Almost all of the hunt for communists in the government and in schools relied on vague accusations and threats to name names. The accusations and the hints of conspiracy were enough to make people afraid.

LARRY TYE, HISTORIAN: He grasped something earlier treason-shouters hadn't: that counting and naming the actual traitors had a frontier justice allure.

FLY ON THE WALL: Frontier justice means taking the law into your own hands, just like what happened to witches. By the time McCarthy flew into Denver the next day, a crowd of reporters was waiting to see the list. McCarthy told them that he would be glad to show it to them, but claimed he had left it in his other suit on the plane.

DENVER POST: Left Commie list in other bag.

FLY ON THE WALL: In Reno, Nevada, the next day, McCarthy gave another speech, this time saying there were fifty-seven communists in the State Department. Confused, reporters invited him for drinks the following week. Round after round, they pressed him for details. By the end Joe was screaming that the newsmen had stolen his list of communists.

FRANK McCULLOCH, REPORTER: He lost his list between his eighth and ninth bourbons.

McCARTHY: I just want you to know I've got a pailful of shit, and I'm going to use it where it does me the most good.

FLY ON THE WALL: After he made his speeches, McCarthy had sent Truman a telegram and released it to the press.

> **McCARTHY:** Your board did a painstaking job and named hundreds which it listed as "dangerous to the security of the nation." . . . I would suggest therefore, Mr. President, that you simply pick up your phone and ask Mr. Acheson [secretary of state] how many of those whom your board has labeled as dangerous he failed to discharge . . . Failure on your part will label the Democratic Party [as] being the bedfellow of international communism.

FLY ON THE WALL: This, from a senator who was such a nobody that he was sent to Wheeling, West Virginia. Livid, Truman dashed off a reply in kind, but never sent it.

> **TRUMAN:** I read your telegram . . . with a great deal of interest. Your telegram is not only . . . an insolent approach to a situation that should have been worked out between man and man but it shows conclusively that you are not even fit to have a hand in the Government of the United States.
>
> I am very sure that the people of Wisconsin are extremely sorry that they are represented by a person who has as little sense of responsibility as you have.

FLY ON THE WALL: Truman controlled his temper enough not to send the telegram, but Joe loved being the center of attention. McCarthy was now more popular than ever. He even got an "ism" attached to his name. In a political cartoon, Herb Block drew a barrel of tar labeled "McCarthyism" atop a wobbly tower of buckets, alluding to the old American tradition of tarring and feathering.

Eventually he would be on the covers of both *Time* and *Newsweek*. McCarthy loved flattery, and he also knew how to hand it out. In 1952, he had said to Hoover:

> **McCARTHY:** No one need ever erect a monument to you. You have built your own monument in the form of the FBI— for the FBI is J Edgar Hoover and I think we can rest assured that it always will be.

FLY ON THE WALL: Now McCarthy needed Hoover's help. McCarthy might have sounded ready to take on the president, but privately, he had a problem. His so-called list was made up of outdated names that he couldn't show anyone. In a panic, he begged J. Edgar Hoover to give him numbers to back up what he had already said. McCarthy admitted to Hoover that he had made the numbers up.

> **HOOVER:** Don't ever use specific figures.

FLY ON THE WALL: Having passed on this advice, Hoover did try to help his protégé.

> **HOOVER:** Review the files and get anything you can for him.

> **WILLIAM SULLIVAN, HOOVER ASSISTANT:** We didn't have enough evidence to show that there was a single communist in the State Department.

FLY ON THE WALL: The Senate began hearings to investigate McCarthy's claims on March 8, 1950. McCarthy soon made it clear that he wasn't going to play by the Senate's rules or anybody's idea of polite behavior. During a four-hour talk on the Senate floor, McCarthy offered to show Herbert Lehman, a seventy-two-year-old Democrat from New York, one of the letters he'd been waving around. Lehman walked over to McCarthy's desk and held out his hand.

LEHMAN: Will the Senator from Wisconsin let me see the letter?

McCARTHY: Does the Senator wish to come close enough to read it?

LEHMAN: I would like to read it in my own way.

McCARTHY: Will the senator sit down?

LEHMAN: May I say, Mr. President—

McCARTHY: I do not yield further at this time.

McCARTHY (GROWLING THIS TIME): Go back to your seat, old man.

STEWART ALSOP, REPORTER IN THE GALLERY: Lehman looked all around the chamber, appealing for support. He was met with silence and lowered eyes. Slowly, he turned and walked . . . back to his seat. "There goes the end of the

Republic," I muttered to my wife. . . . The silence of the
Senate that evening was a measure of the fear which McCarthy
inspired in almost all politicians . . . Old Senator Lehman's
back, waddling off in retreat, seemed to symbolize the final
defeat of decency.

FLY ON THE WALL: Only one senator stood up to McCarthy:
Margaret Chase Smith, a Republican from Maine, the only woman in
the Senate. She drafted a Declaration of Conscience and got six of her
moderate colleagues to cosponsor it. She ran into McCarthy minutes
before she took the Senate floor to talk about the declaration.

McCARTHY: Margaret, you look very serious. Are you going to make a speech?

SMITH: Yes, and you will not like it.

McCARTHY (SMILING): Is it about me?

SMITH: Yes, but I'm not going to mention your name.

FLY ON THE WALL: The worst thing you could do to McCarthy was not mention his name.

> **SMITH:** I would like to speak briefly and simply about a serious national condition . . . I speak as a woman. I speak as a United States senator. I speak as an American. . . .
>
> Those of us who shout the loudest about Americanism in making character assassinations are all too frequently those who, by our own words and acts, ignore some of the basic principles of Americanism—
>
> The right to criticize.
>
> The right to hold unpopular beliefs.
>
> The right to protest.
>
> The right of independent thought.
>
> The exercise of these rights should not cost one single American citizen his reputation or livelihood . . .
>
> As an American, I don't want a Democratic administration "whitewash" or "coverup" any more than I want a Republican smear or witch hunt.

FLY ON THE WALL: When she finished speaking, the room was mostly silent. A few senators congratulated her. No one seemed to notice that

McCarthy had left the chamber without saying anything. McCarthy didn't attack her to her face . . . but that didn't mean he didn't attack. He preferred attacking people in the press. He sneered at Smith, calling her and her supporters Snow White and the Six Dwarfs. One by one, five of the six senators who had signed her Declaration of Conscience backed off. Margaret Chase Smith was deeply offended. In the end, only one remained at her side.

DUCK AND COVER: RUSSIA GETS THE BOMB

TRUMAN: We have evidence that within recent weeks an atomic explosion occurred in the USSR.

NEW YORK *SUN*: Truman Says Russia Set Off Atom Blast.

WASHINGTON *EVENING STAR*: Truman Reports Atomic Blast in Russia.

FLY ON THE WALL: The American public was shocked. How could Russia have gotten the bomb? It could only have happened because the Russians had stolen our secrets.

DAVID MUNNS, HISTORIAN: Part of America's obsession with hunting for communists was that nobody could believe that the Russians had scientists who would have been capable of the bomb, even though it was obvious that they did.

FLY ON THE WALL: People were scared that the Russians having the atom bomb could lead to World War III. Schools began to hold bomb drills in case communist enemies dropped an atom bomb on American soil. In order not to terrify kids, a film with a cartoon turtle named Bert helped show schoolkids how to survive.

> **FILM NARRATOR:** We all know the atomic bomb is very dangerous. Since it may be used against us, we must get ready for it . . . You'll know when it comes . . . There is a bright flash, brighter than the sun, brighter than anything you've ever seen. If you are not ready and did not know what to do, then it could hurt you in different ways . . . First you duck. Then you cover.

FLY ON THE WALL: That means you hide under your desk.

> **BERT THE TURTLE:** Remember what to do, friends. Now tell me right out loud. What are you supposed to do when you see the flash?

> **ELIZABETH LEVY, AUTHOR, REMEMBERING HER GRADE SCHOOL:** We had nuclear bomb drills in Buffalo, New York. We were told to cover the back of our neck with our hands and make sure our face was tucked away. We were also given a sheet to cover ourselves in the gym. We were taught that would save us from radiation. I thought if I held it tight, I'd be okay.

> **ANDREA BALIS, AUTHOR, TALKING ABOUT HER GRADE SCHOOL:** My school had a pamphlet they issued to

all the parents that told them where to find our dead bodies (presumably under the desk or under the table in the cafeteria) after a nuclear attack. I was terrified.

FLY ON THE WALL: J. Edgar Hoover was obsessed with proving that he could save America from communist spies. Hoover caught a spy and leaked the information to the press even before she was arrested. She was a young woman named Judith Coplon, who was an employee of the Department of Justice. The problem was that Hoover wanted the headlines, but he couldn't let anyone know how he had found out about it.

United States intelligence agents had broken a Soviet code they called Venona during World War II. They kept it secret from everybody so that the Soviets would keep using the same code. The actual labor was done by a group of women who worked in an abandoned girls' school in Arlington, Virginia.

SMITHSONIAN MAGAZINE: The Venona messages were encoded in a fiendishly complex system.

ESPIONAGE AGAINST THE UNITED STATES BY AMERICAN CITIZENS 1947-2001: According to transcripts of Soviet wartime cables deciphered by the National Security Agency in the Venona project, code names of some 350 cooperating Americans appear in the Soviet wartime cable traffic.

FLY ON THE WALL: The Soviet wartime cables revealed a female agent with the code name Sima working at the Justice Department.

KGB MEMO: She gives the impression of a very serious, modest, thoughtful young woman who is ideologically close to us.

FLY ON THE WALL: The FBI wanted to identify Judith Coplon as Sima, but agents couldn't prove it without revealing that the Venona code had been cracked. So they started tapping her phones. Wiretapping without a judge's authority is not legal. Hoover did it anyhow.

ELLEN SCHRECKER AND PHILLIP DEERY, HISTORIANS: The Venona documents themselves, while of undoubted historical significance, are fragmentary, and . . . Venona should be read with circumspection rather than reverence . . . [remembering that it was] . . . in the self-interest of local KGB officers to inflate the importance of their intelligence reports to Moscow.

FLY ON THE WALL: Judith Coplon was arrested in March 1949. The FBI used the illegal wiretap evidence in Coplon's trial, and she was found guilty. But on appeal, when it came out that the evidence had been illegally obtained, her conviction was overturned. The appeals court did not dismiss the espionage charges, however, and sent her case back to be retried.

EMILY SOCOLOV, JUDITH COPLON'S DAUGHTER:
It wasn't until seventeen years later that the charges were thrown out. My mother couldn't vote; she couldn't drive. When we took a trip, I never knew why she couldn't go with us. When I was growing up, my mother and father taught us family loyalty was one of the most important values we could have . . . Loyalty. Loyalty, which is ironic when you think of loyalties . . . tests and all that was going on. They wanted us to have as normal a childhood as we could.

BOB LAMPHERE, FBI AGENT: Nothing that happened in the entire Coplon affair—especially in the reversal of the conviction—pleased Director Hoover.

POLICE ACTION IN KOREA

FLY ON THE WALL: Russian communists now had the bomb. China was a communist country too. Would anything stop communism? If one country was infected, the next would fall. This became known as the domino theory. The idea is simple. It's like when people line up dominoes close enough so that when you push one, they all fall down. There's no stopping it once it starts. Americans began to see communism like a disease, something you could catch.

> **GALLUP POLLS, 1950:** Seventy percent of Americans think the Soviet Union is trying to rule the world. Seventy-three percent think American cities would be bombed in a world war. Nineteen percent think another world war would mean the end of humankind.

FLY ON THE WALL: On June 25, 1950, it looked like the dominoes were starting to fall and Korea was the next to go down. Most American citizens weren't sure where exactly Korea was, but at the end of World War II, the Western Allies decided to split Korea along the

38th parallel, effectively splitting the country in two. That's not what the Koreans wanted. They wanted a united country. But North Korea became a Soviet-supported regime, and the United States and its allies supported the government of South Korea.

NEW YORK *DAILY NEWS***:** N. Korea Reds Declare War: Invade South by Land and Sea.

FLY ON THE WALL: Truman had a dilemma. The United States had promised South Korea its support. But Truman knew Americans had had enough of war, so instead he pushed the United Nations to declare a "police action" to stop communist China. The war was taking place in Korea, but it was really a fight between the United States and communist forces backed by China and the Soviet Union.

SECRETARY OF STATE DEAN ACHESON: If the best minds in the world had set out to find us the worst possible location in the world to fight this damnable war, politically and militarily, the unanimous choice would have been Korea!

CHARLES RANGEL, BLACK SOLDIER WHO BECAME A CONGRESSMAN: I was a high school dropout. I was seventeen. I had no idea where Korea was. They said it was a "police action." I thought it would be like a little riot in Harlem.

FLY ON THE WALL: Letters home from Korea soon convinced Americans that just as in World War II, American soldiers were being sacrificed for somebody else.

ARDEN ROWLEY, SOLDIER IN KOREA: It was so cold that you could spit, and it would freeze before it hit the

ground . . . It was so cold that if you touched your bare hand on a metallic object, it would stick there . . . Many soldiers, if they were wounded, and couldn't be taken care of right away, would freeze to death.

FLY ON THE WALL: General Douglas MacArthur, the hero of the Pacific in World War II, was the general stationed closest to Korea. He was picked to lead the United Nations forces, including American troops. The problem was that Douglas MacArthur was in no way interested in diplomacy, only military force, and he had no respect for Harry Truman, whom he regarded as a nobody. He was seventy years old in 1950, and he was somebody who believed in his own greatness.

> **TRUMAN (JUNE 1945):** What to do with Mr. Prima Donna, Brass Hat, Five Star MacArthur . . . Mac tells God right off. It is a very great pity that we have to have stuffed shirts like that in key positions.

> **GENERAL DWIGHT EISENHOWER (JANUARY 1942):** MacArthur is as big a baby as ever . . . He still likes his boot lickers.

FLY ON THE WALL: At first in Korea, MacArthur seemed to be as brilliant a general as he had been in World War II. But what MacArthur didn't understand was that this was an entirely different kind of war. It wasn't the kind where you could bomb a country into submission. This war was being fought by guerilla fighters, on their own ground, who wanted their country back, and they knew their country much better than any Western troops would ever know it.

CHARLES RANGEL:

When the Chinese hit, for three days they talked to us in perfect English, telling us to surrender, that it was not our war, that we were black troops, and we were not treated equally . . . There were so many soldiers that froze to death because they fell asleep.

ARDEN ROWLEY:

The communist forces had completely surrounded the division . . . [We] became prisoners of war . . . As we marched to this camp, many men's feet froze. I remember one sergeant lost all ten of his toes and [they] chopped the bones off his feet with a pair of hedge trimmers.

FLY ON THE WALL: Even though three hundred thousand Chinese troops—who MacArthur had said would never attack—had overwhelmed his men, MacArthur was not the kind of a general who would admit a mistake. Instead, he wanted to drop atom bombs on mainland cities of China and Manchuria. Truman was furious. The one thing he was not going to do was start World War III.

TRUMAN: I was ready to kick him into the North China Sea at that time. I was never so put out in my life.

FLY ON THE WALL: Truman fired MacArthur because MacArthur ignored direct orders from his commander in chief (President Truman himself) and pushed troops farther into North Korea. Truman knew people would be angry because MacArthur was a popular general and hero. But Truman was never afraid to take the heat for a decision that might be unpopular. On his desk Truman kept a sign saying THE BUCK STOPS HERE!, which had been made for him by prisoners in Oklahoma.

THE ROSENBERG SPY CASE

FLY ON THE WALL: With no faith in their president, and their boys far away in a godforsaken place, many Americans believed that communists had already sneaked into America and were hiding among them.

Just a few months into the Korean War, in September 1950, Congress passed the McCarran Internal Security Act, forcing registration of all "Communist-action" and "Communist front" organizations. The McCarran Act magnified Americans' fear of outsiders. It allowed for the detention and deportation of suspected subversive elements.

It was named after Senator Patrick McCarran, a Democrat from Nevada who supported Joe McCarthy's actions. *U.S. News and World Report* talked with him about communist infiltration after the law was passed.

QUESTION: Has this infiltration gone on in all walks of life? For example, do you think there's been infiltration in the press?

McCARRAN: Oh, yes.

QUESTION: How about the churches?

McCARRAN: Yes, all kinds of churches.

QUESTION: How about educational institutions?

McCARRAN: Yes, if you mean faculties [the teachers].

QUESTION: How about labor unions?

McCARRAN: Oh, yes.

DAVID OSHINSKY: The McCarran Act reflected a war mentality that equated dissent with treason . , . Truman vetoed it. His stand took great courage. It would have been easy to give in and sign something that the public clearly wanted.

TRUMAN: [Communists] are noisy and they are trouble-some, but they are not a major threat.

FLY ON THE WALL: The House overrode his veto, 286–48. The Senate battled over it for twenty-two hours, and then overrode it, 57–10.

The fear of communists living among regular Americans became all too real with the arrest of Julius Rosenberg, who lived in an apartment in New York with his wife, Ethel, and their two boys, Robby, three, and Michael, seven.

JEAN LE BEC, CHILDHOOD FRIEND OF THE ROSENBERG CHILDREN: Ethel and Jules were just another of my parents' friends. There were a whole group of them—they would meet at Bear Mountain State Park in the Catskills. Robby and Michael were just two of the kids we played with. We'd have deviled eggs and pineapple upside-down cake. We loved it because the adults forgot about us during the day. At night, we'd all sing and dance—Ethel had a beautiful singing voice.

MICHAEL MEEROPOL, ELDER SON OF ROSENBERGS:
On July 17, 1950, while Robby was asleep and I listened to *The Lone Ranger*, the FBI came to our apartment to arrest our father . . . An FBI man turned off the radio. I turned it on; he turned it off again. We kept this up until I finally gave in.

FLY ON THE WALL: Julius Rosenberg was arrested on suspicion of espionage. His wife, Ethel, was arrested a month later. They were accused of passing secrets about the atom bomb.

> **DAVID MUNNS, HISTORIAN:** None of the "secrets" really were important to the Russians' knowledge of how to make the bomb. Most of them they already knew.

FLY ON THE WALL: In March 1951, in the middle of the Korean War, the Rosenbergs were put on trial.

> **JEAN LE BEC:** After the Rosenbergs were arrested, everything changed. My sister and I, and all the kids, like Robby and Michael—we had played games of good guys and bad guys. And we were always the good guys. Now were we the bad guys? My parents and their friends became much more serious, and everything was quiet as if there were very big secrets.

FLY ON THE WALL: The problem for the government was that the case against the Rosenbergs was also based on the Venona cables, and Hoover and the government still could not make them public. Hoover was very anxious to make an example of the Rosenbergs to prove what a good spy catcher he was. Enter Roy Cohn, a very young prosecutor with political pull. He was only twenty-three and was given the plum job of cross-examining witnesses at the trial.

> **DAVE MARCUS, ROY COHN'S COUSIN:** Roy looked scary to me as a kid. He had hooded eyes and dark shadows under

his eyes. When he talked, his tongue would dart in and out of his mouth like a snake.

FLY ON THE WALL: Both Rosenbergs were found guilty. Hoover and Cohn wanted the judge to give Ethel and Julius Rosenberg the death penalty. And he did.

BOB LAMPHERE, FBI AGENT: We didn't want them to die. We wanted them to talk—confess and possibly implicate others in the ring.

JEAN LE BEC: I remember my sister waking me up and telling me that they were going to kill the Rosenbergs. Because they had lied about big secrets—and I was scared to death. I had lied. I had lied about not feeling well to stay home from school . . . or I had lied and blamed my sister for something I had done.

I LIKE IKE

McCARTHY: We can elect a real *American* President in 1952.

FLY ON THE WALL: The presidential elections had everybody excited. Americans were sick of the war in Korea and angry at a president who had let spies steal our secrets. Truman's approval rating was at his lowest yet, 22 percent, and he announced that he would not seek reelection. For the first time in twenty-four years, two new candidates would be running for president.

Both parties were looking around for someone who could win. Both parties wanted Dwight Eisenhower, the hero of World War II. The problem was that nobody knew what party he belonged to.

EISENHOWER: Anybody is a damn fool if he actually seeks to be President.

FLY ON THE WALL: And for a while, there was some speculation that Senator Joseph McCarthy would run for president. But the Republican establishment thought McCarthy was a loose cannon. As William Rogers, who became Eisenhower's attorney general, later wrote about McCarthy when he was running for re-election to the Senate:

WILLIAM ROGERS, DEPUTY ATTORNEY GENERAL: Joe never plans a damn thing, he doesn't know from one week to the next, not even from one day to the next, what he's going to be doing . . . He just hits out in any direction, no plan, no forethought.

FLY ON THE WALL: The Republicans pursued Eisenhower relentlessly. Finally, while still in Europe as commander of the military forces of the North Atlantic Treaty Organization, Eisenhower let the Republicans enter his name into the New Hampshire primary. Eisenhower was famous for his easy charm and his ability to get people to work together. After all, he had gotten all the generals during World War II to cooperate. Without even showing up, he won in New Hampshire. He was the opposite of Joe McCarthy in every way.

EISENHOWER (JUNE 12, 1945): Humility must always be the portion of any man who receives acclaim earned in the blood of his followers and the sacrifices of his friends.

FLY ON THE WALL: Even though Eisenhower won the Republican nomination, McCarthy was the star of the convention. The Republicans gave him a prime-time speaking slot.

McCARTHY: My good friends, I say one Communist in a defense plant is one Communist too many.

Applause.

McCARTHY: One Communist on the faculty of one university is one Communist too many. . . .

Applause.

McCARTHY: And even if there were only one Communist in the State Department, that would still be one Communist too many.

Applause.

MILES McMILLIN, REPORTER: He is getting skilled advice on the use of television. TV people said that he was the only speaker on the convention program to wear make-up.

FLY ON THE WALL: Eisenhower was the nominee, and his running mate was Richard Nixon from California, who had come into the Senate in the same freshman class as Joe McCarthy. To millions of Americans watching on that hot day in July 1952, McCarthy was still their hero, saying things that others were afraid to. McCarthy had enough power that the Republican Party platform reflected many of his positions.

REPUBLICAN PARTY PLATFORM (1952): A Republican President will appoint only persons of unquestioned loyalty.

FLY ON THE WALL: Part of Eisenhower's success as a general was that he could get along with all sorts of people. One strategy was that he didn't trash people in public. And Eisenhower knew that Joe McCarthy was still adored by many of his Wisconsin constituents.

REPORTER: Do you favor the reelection of Senator Joseph McCarthy of Wisconsin?

WISCONSIN FARMHAND: Yes, I guess almost everybody in this part of the country is for McCarthy. He's against communism—and we're against communism. Besides, if he wasn't telling the truth they'd 'a' hung him long ago.

WISCONSIN POLITICIAN: Joe treats the Communist party member as someone to be dealt with via the fist. He's a slugger.

FLY ON THE WALL: Eisenhower was far too smart a politician to attack McCarthy directly.

EISENHOWER: I shall say again that I am not going to indulge in any kind of [talk about] personalities under any pretext whatsoever . . . No one could be more determined than I that any kind of communistic, subversive, or pinkish influence be uprooted from responsible places in our government.

FLY ON THE WALL: But privately, Eisenhower made no secret of what he thought of Joe McCarthy. Eisenhower later described McCarthy as a . . .

EISENHOWER: Pimple on [the] path of progress.

FLY ON THE WALL: Eisenhower's Democratic opponent was the governor of Illinois, Adlai Stevenson. Although Stevenson was eloquent and witty, he had his handicaps. He was divorced, which in 1952 was shocking. Even worse to many voters, Stevenson had vetoed an Illinois bill that would have made state employees take a loyalty oath.

STEVENSON: The whole notion of loyalty inquisitions is a natural characteristic of the police state, not of democracy . . . We must not burn down the house to kill the rats.

FLY ON THE WALL: McCarthy was dying for a chance to take on Stevenson, but Eisenhower wanted McCarthy as far away from his campaign as possible. McCarthy linked Stevenson with the communist newspaper *Daily Worker*. As McCarthy was flying around the country, campaigning for himself and other Republicans, he was drinking heavily. Some mornings, he ordered nothing for breakfast except a glass of whiskey, into which he poured a tablespoon of orange juice. One reporter later saw him swallow a half stick of butter in one bite.

SAM SHAFFER, JOURNALIST: What the hell are you doing?

McCARTHY: Oh, this helps me hold my liquor better.

FLY ON THE WALL: This was the first election in which television advertising became important. And Eisenhower's easy grin gave people a feeling that everything was going to be okay. He was helped by top-notch advertising that included animated commercials made by Disney.

"I Like Ike" was the animated commercial for Republican presidential candidate Dwight D. Eisenhower in 1952.

FLY ON THE WALL: The results were that Eisenhower won big, and his coattails were long enough that Republicans took control of both the Senate and the House of Representatives.

AN EXECUTION

FLY ON THE WALL: No sooner did Eisenhower take office than he had to face one of the ultimate tests for a president—life or death. He was faced with the decision of whether or not to let the Rosenbergs' execution go forward. Only he as president could grant clemency and reduce their sentence. There was an international outcry against the execution to spare their lives.

> **DOROTHY DAY, CATHOLIC JOURNALIST:** Let us have no part with the vindictive State and let us pray for Ethel and Julius Rosenberg.

FLY ON THE WALL: The Rosenbergs had been held separately in solitary confinement for three years. People picketed the White House, begging Eisenhower to save their lives. Robby and Michael wrote Eisenhower a letter.

Eisenhower was caught between sympathy for the children and what he saw as his duty.

Dear Mr. President,
Please don't leave my
brother and I without a
mommy and daddy.
They have always been
good to us. We love them
very much.
Michael and Robert
Rosenberg
36 Laurel Hill Terrace
New York, N.Y.

EISENHOWER: The execution of two human beings is a grave matter. But even graver is the thought of the millions of dead whose deaths may be directly attributable to what these spies have done . . . I will not intervene in this matter.

FLY ON THE WALL: Roy Cohn, the ambitious young prosecutor, with the support of Hoover and the FBI, had led the demands for the execution of both Julius and Ethel Rosenberg. Later, it was revealed that he just viewed the death penalty as a way to make the Rosenbergs talk.

ALAN DERSHOWITZ, LAWYER: Just because Julius Rosenberg was guilty of spying for the Soviet Union does not mean that he was not also framed. It certainly does not mean that his wife was not framed. . . . I asked Cohn how he felt about his role more than 30 years later.

ROY COHN: Great.

FLY ON THE WALL: In Sing Sing prison in New York, Ethel Rosenberg wrote her sons one final letter.

ETHEL ROSENBERG: Dearest sweethearts, my most precious children, . . . We wish we might have had the tremendous joy and gratification of living our lives out with you. Your daddy who is with me in the last momentous hours, sends his heart and all the love that is in it for his dearest boys . . . We press you close and kiss you with all our strength.

Lovingly, Daddy and Mommy

FLY ON THE WALL: Robby and Michael Rosenberg were eventually adopted by Abel and Anne Meeropol, who were activists for social justice. Under a pen name, Abel Meeropol had written the song "Strange Fruit," about the lynching of Black people in the South.

UNITED PRESS (JUNE 20, 1953): Their lips defiantly sealed to the end, the husband and wife spy team went to their death in Sing Sing's electric chair shortly before sundown.

BATMAN GETS HIS ROBIN, AND ROBIN GETS HIS ROBIN

FLY ON THE WALL: Many people were deeply saddened by the execution of the Rosenbergs, but for others it opened up opportunity. McCarthy had been warning of homegrown communists, and here they were. His triumph did not please everyone. Many in the Republican establishment believed or hoped that McCarthy would fade away now that his party, for the first time in over twenty years, held both houses of Congress and the presidency. McCarthy was now the chair of the Committee on Government Operations.

> **McCARTHY:** Some people don't realize it, but that committee could be the most powerful in the Senate. I can investigate anybody who ever received money from the government, and that covers a lot of ground.

FLY ON THE WALL: The committee would get a lot more famous once McCarthy hired Rosenberg prosecutor Roy Cohn to be the subcommittee's chief counsel.

JOE McCARTHY: Roy is one of the most brilliant young men I have ever met.

RUTH WATT, CHIEF CLERK OF THE SUBCOMMITTEE ON INVESTIGATIONS: [My impression of Roy Cohn was that] he was going so fast that I couldn't keep up with him.

FLY ON THE WALL: Then Cohn hired G. David Schine, a twenty-five-year-old Harvard man who had caught his eye.

HARVARD CRIMSON:

Wealth, of course, is not out of place here, but Schine, certainly one of the richest men in his class, made it so. He [had] . . . an exquisitely furnished room, a valet [and] a big black convertible equipped with a two-way phone-radio [very, very rare in 1949].

TIME MAGAZINE:

Dave Schine turned out to be a pleasant, articulate young man, with the build and features of a junior-grade Greek god . . . Dave wanted to be a Communist investigator, and he regarded Roy as just about the smartest man he ever knew.

WATT: Dave was never on the payroll. He was just a consultant on his own. A sidelight on that . . . Dave wrote a letter to the Rules Committee saying that it would be very desirous if Dave Schine could go in the senators' baths and so on, and he signed Joe McCarthy's name on it. Of course the Rules Committee turned it down flat, and Senator McCarthy knew nothing about it until later.

FLY ON THE WALL: Cohn and Schine moved into the Schine family's luxurious suite at the Waldorf-Astoria Hotel in New York. McCarthy asked them to help with hearings into the State Department's information programs, such as the Voice for America's Libraries in capitals around the world. McCarthy's hearings sent the State Department's International Information Administration, which oversaw the libraries and information programs, into a panic.

IIA BULLETIN: In order to avoid all misunderstanding, no repeat no materials by any Communists, fellow-travelers, etc. will be used under any circumstances by any IIA media.

FLY ON THE WALL: Nobody knew what the "et cetera" meant. Hundreds of books were discarded, some burned, many by Black writers, whether they were known communists or not, such as the well-known poet Langston Hughes and Walter White, head of the NAACP. Cohn and Schine didn't trust the librarians, though. They decided to fly to Europe and personally inspect the libraries run by the U.S. State Department there.

FRANCIS WILCOX, SENATE FOREIGN RELATIONS COMMITTEE CHIEF OF STAFF: The staff was very apprehensive about Cohn and Schine going abroad and engaging in all kinds of irresponsible behavior, bringing discredit to our country, to our foreign policy, and to the idea of the professional staff.

FLY ON THE WALL: Cohn and Schine landed in Paris. In the next eighteen days, they flew from Paris to Bonn, to Berlin, to Munich, then on to Vienna, Belgrade, Athens, and Rome. From there, it was back to Paris, then on to London, the final stop. The British press was not impressed.

FINANCIAL TIMES, LONDON: Scummy snoopers.

MANCHESTER GUARDIAN: Their limited vocabulary, their self-complacency, and their paucity of ideas, coupled with the immense power they wield, had the effect of drawing much sympathy for all ranks of the United States Diplomatic Service who have to submit to this sort of thing.

DREW PEARSON, AMERICAN COLUMNIST: The two junior G-men, now known as Mc-men, have denied that Schine hit Cohn on the head with a rolled-up magazine in the hotel corridor or that the chambermaid later found their room turned topsy-turvy.

FLY ON THE WALL: The hijinks were funny, but to the people being threatened it wasn't funny. Even suspicion of helping communists could ruin careers and lives. Raymond Kaplan, a radio engineer for Voice of America, which was one of the State Department programs being investigated by McCarthy, threw himself in front of a speeding truck in Massachusetts, leaving a handwritten note for his wife and child.

KAPLAN: Once the dogs are set on you, everything you have done since the beginning of time is suspect.

FLY ON THE WALL: The suicides and the book burnings shocked many people, and more and more newspapers began questioning McCarthy's tactics.

> **JOSEPH AND STEWART ALSOP, COLUMNISTS:** The State Department's book-burning program, undertaken in craven fear of Senator Joseph R. McCarthy, . . . [is a] cowardly knuckling under to the political yahoos.

> **COHN (IN 1968):** [The trip] was a colossal mistake . . . David Schine and I unwittingly handed Joe McCarthy's enemies a perfect opportunity to spread the tale that a couple of young, inexperienced clowns were bustling about Europe, ordering State Department officials around, burning books, creating chaos wherever they went, and disrupting foreign relations.

FLY ON THE WALL: Eisenhower privately despised McCarthy.

> **EISENHOWER (IN HIS DIARY):** Senator McCarthy is, of course, so anxious for the headlines that he is prepared to go to any extremes in order to secure some mention of his name in the public press . . . I really believe that nothing will be so effective in combating his particular kind of trouble-making as to ignore him. This he cannot stand.

FLY ON THE WALL: Finally, at Dartmouth College's commencement before an audience of ten thousand, Eisenhower made his feelings known without mentioning McCarthy by name.

EISENHOWER: Don't join the book burners. Don't think you are going to conceal faults by concealing evidence that they ever existed. Don't be afraid to go into your libraries and read every book . . . How will we defeat communism unless we know what it is, and what it teaches?

THE LAVENDER SCARE

FLY ON THE WALL: The reality was that even though the "McCarthy boys" had garnered some bad headlines, McCarthy himself had never been more popular.

SENATOR LYNDON B. JOHNSON, DEMOCRAT FROM TEXAS: He's the sorriest senator up here. Can't tie his goddamn shoes. But he's riding high now. He's got people scared to death some Communist will strangle 'em in their sleep, and anybody who takes him on before the fevers cool—well, you don't get in a pissin' contest with a polecat.

FLY ON THE WALL: Many of the people closest to President Eisenhower urged him to go after McCarthy.

MILTON EISENHOWER, THE PRESIDENT'S BROTHER: McCarthy was such an evil and penetrating force in our society that I wanted the president, in the strongest possible language, to repudiate him.

PRESIDENT EISENHOWER: You want me to make a martyr of McCarthy and get the whole Senate to stand behind him just because a President has attacked him?

MILTON EISENHOWER: [My brother] loathed McCarthy as much as any human being could possibly loathe another . . . He felt McCarthy was a curse on the American scene.

FLY ON THE WALL: The president did write a letter to the American Library Association. It was read aloud at the association's annual conference.

PRESIDENT EISENHOWER: Our librarians serve the precious liberties of our nation: freedom of inquiry, freedom of the spoken and the written word, freedom of exchange of ideas . . . A democracy smugly disdainful of new ideas would be a sick democracy. A democracy chronically fearful of new ideas would be a dying democracy . . . There are some zealots who—with more wrath than wisdom—would adopt a strangely unintelligent course . . . As it is an ancient truth that freedom cannot be legislated into existence, so it is no less obvious that freedom cannot be censored into existence.

FLY ON THE WALL: This is the dilemma of Eisenhower. He could make great speeches about freedom, but he didn't always stand up completely for the forces that fought for civil rights and personal liberty. Eisenhower was being pressured to prove to Americans that he could be even tougher on communists and communist sympathizers than McCarthy.

Hoover insisted to Eisenhower that homosexuals were a security threat as much as communists—this despite constant rumors about

Hoover's own homosexuality. Eisenhower issued an executive order that would apply to all federal employees.

EXECUTIVE ORDER 10450: WHEREAS the interests of the national security require that all persons privileged to be employed in the departments and agencies of the Government, shall be reliable, trustworthy, of good conduct and character, and of complete and unswerving loyalty to the United States, . . . it is hereby ordered as follows: . . . The appointment of each . . . employee . . . shall be made subject to investigation . . . The investigations . . . shall relate but not be limited to . . . any criminal, infamous, dishonest, immoral, or notoriously disgraceful conduct, habitual use of intoxicants to excess, drug addiction, sexual perversion [and] . . . any facts which furnish reason to believe that the individual may be subjected to coercion, influence, or pressure which may cause him to act contrary to the best interests of the national security.

MAX LERNER, JOURNALIST: J. Edgar Hoover says [homosexuals] are more vulnerable [to blackmail].

FLY ON THE WALL: Under Eisenhower, the loyalty boards that Truman had set up took on even more power. Now they could fire anyone who worked for the government who behaved suspiciously. But their idea of suspicious was very broad indeed. Soon every homosexual was seen as a threat to the morals and security of the nation in the Lavender Scare, a term author and historian David Johnson later popularized. Homosexuals in the State Department had been under threat in the 1940s and 1950s, but Eisenhower made it an official policy.

SENATOR KENNETH WHERRY, REPUBLICAN FROM NEBRASKA: Who could be more dangerous to the United States of America than a pervert, who is in the most vulnerable position to be blackmailed into giving information?

EUGENE D. WILLIAMS, SPECIAL ASSISTANT ATTORNEY GENERAL OF CALIFORNIA (1949): All too often we lose sight of the fact that the homosexual is an inveterate seducer of the young of both sexes, and that he presents a social problem because he is not content with being degenerate himself; he must have degenerate companions.

FLY ON THE WALL: This is an argument that is sometimes made even though there is zero evidence to back it up.

WHERRY: I shall continue as an American citizen and as the junior Senator from Nebraska to do everything I can to clean out moral perverts and subversives from Government.

FLY ON THE WALL: Hoover kept on cranking out "sexual deviant" accusations and feeding the information to McCarthy. Hoover kept 330,000 pages of documents on suspected homosexuals. On the Senate floor, Joe McCarthy took up the drumbeat.

McCARTHY: I asked one of our top intelligence men in Washington, one day, "Why do you find men who are so fanatically Communist? Is there something about the Communist philosophy that attracts them?" He said, "Senator McCarthy, if you had been in this work as long as we have been, you would realize that there is something wrong with each one of these individuals. You will find that practically every active Communist is twisted mentally or physically in some way."

FLY ON THE WALL: Of course, McCarthy likely made up the encounter. But many, many real people lost their jobs over such accusations. Along with the thousands who were forced out of the government over the years, plenty of others found their careers shortened or dead-ended, just because of rumors. Many people who were not ordinarily fearful became frightened.

CAPTAIN JOAN CASSIDY, U.S. NAVY (RETIRED): They swooped in like Death with his scythe, sweeping through the place and knocking everybody out, every one of the women. They pulled them out of bed in the middle of the night . . . and started questioning them about their sex life and whether they were gay. And it was by association . . . They said to them, "We have your friend in the next room. She's already told us that you're gay, so you might as well give us the names of others." . . . They were going to discharge them, and we heard that they also sent letters home telling their parents why . . . If they did that to me, how would I ever face my family? . . . I couldn't do it, I just couldn't do it. It was too big a chance to take. I had to give up the possibility of admiral because I was gay and because I wasn't sure if I could hide it well enough.

FLY ON THE WALL: It wasn't only government workers who were in danger of being fired because of rumors that they were gay. Bayard Rustin, the black civil rights activist and a mentor of Martin Luther King Jr., was forced out of his position in the Southern Christian Leadership Conference.

WALTER NAEGLE, RUSTIN'S PARTNER: Bayard was comfortable with being gay—but he was always having obstacles thrown in his way. The struggle for justice is never finished—[there is] always a new cause, new incident to address . . . Long before Rosa Parks, Bayard refused to get to the back of the bus. It hurt him that other black leaders asked him to stay in the background because he was gay.

BAYARD RUSTIN: Dr. King came from a very protected background. I don't think he'd ever known a gay person in his life. . . . Dr. King was never happy about my leaving. He was deeply torn.

FLY ON THE WALL: Frank Kameny was working as an astronomer for the Army Map Service when he was targeted.

EDWARD SHILS, SOCIOLOGIST: Scientists and their friends for a long time stood practically alone in their criticism of the loyalty-security policy . . . Partly because what they do is so important to the national military security, . . . scientists (and higher civil servants) have come to bear the brunt of loyalty-security measures.

DAVID JOHNSON, HISTORIAN: It was no accident that the first federal employee fired for homosexuality to launch a sustained fight with the government was a scientist.

FLY ON THE WALL: Government bureaucrats called Kameny in for an interview.

BUREAUCRATS: We have information which leads us to believe that you are a homosexual. Do you have any comment?

KAMENY: What's the information?

BUREAUCRATS: We can't tell you.

KAMENY: Well, then I can't give you an answer. You don't deserve it. And in any case, this is none of your business.

FLY ON THE WALL: Kameny appealed his firing, beginning a long and ultimately successful legal battle for gay rights. He charged that homosexuals were being treated as second-class citizens.

JOSEPH AND STEWART ALSOP, *SATURDAY EVENING POST*: Why has Washington gone crazy? . . . That sexual perversion presents a clear and present danger to the security of the United States . . . [is] a vulgar folly.

McCARTHY (IN LETTER TO *SATURDAY EVENING POST*): I know some of your editorial staff and frankly can't believe that . . . the long overdue task of removing perverts from our Government would be considered either "vulgar" or "nauseating" to them. I can understand, of course, why it would be considered "vulgar" and "nauseating" by Joe Alsop.

ELIZABETH WINTHROP, DAUGHTER OF STEWART ALSOP AND NIECE OF JOSEPH: My father and uncle told me stories. They were up in the gallery when McCarthy

called them all sorts of names—called them homosexual—then when they were leaving, my father felt someone clap him on the shoulder. It was McCarthy. My father said it felt like someone had smeared him with dirt . . . Both my father and uncle were ardent anticommunists; they just despised Joe McCarthy's tactics. My uncle was a homosexual, but he had to keep it secret. In this day and age—your heart breaks—and what a different man my uncle would have been.

I LOVE LUCY AND *SEE IT NOW*

FLY ON THE WALL: Eisenhower's first months in office were not easy. In addition to his other problems, he had made an election promise to end the war in Korea. In July he was able to keep it.

> **EISENHOWER (JULY 26, 1953):** Tonight we greet, with prayers of thanksgiving, the official news that an armistice was signed almost an hour ago in Korea.

FLY ON THE WALL: Peace in Korea meant that just like after World War II, factories could stop making tanks and start making cars. People suddenly had money in their pockets. They wanted all kinds of things. Toys, clothes, and especially cars and TVs. At the start of the 1950s, there were only three million TVs across America, but by 1959, there were fifty-five million.

Every week most of them were tuned in to watch Lucille Ball in *I Love Lucy*. The show was so popular that on January 19, 1953, more than forty-four million households, 71.7 percent of all households in the country with a TV, tuned in to see Lucy Ricardo give birth to Little Ricky. Later in 1953 actress Lucille Ball testified voluntarily before the

House Un-American Activities Committee. Seventeen years earlier, she had signed up to vote and registered for the Communist Party.

LUCILLE BALL: We had a very bad feeling we had done that. I always felt I would be all right if I didn't vote it, just to appease grandpa.

FLY ON THE WALL: Ball was cleared of suspicion. Remarkably, it didn't hurt her popularity at all. *I Love Lucy* remained the most-watched show on television.

DARIN STRAUSS, NOVELIST: The nation's reservoirs dipped whenever *I Love Lucy* broke for a commercial. A whole country, flushing as one.

GEORGE J. VAN DORP, TOLEDO, OHIO, WATER COMMISSIONER: While *I Love Lucy* is being shown, pressure in the main is consistently high. As soon as the commercial comes on, the pressure drops because people are using the bathroom or whatever . . . When the show is over and people once again avail themselves of water services, the pressure sometimes drops as much as thirty percent.

FLY ON THE WALL: The fact that the country cared more about laughing with Lucy than whether she was a communist was proof to many that McCarthy's brand of anticommunism was finally running out of steam. Joe McCarthy thought that TV would be great for him—after all, he loved the spotlight. But on TV, McCarthy looked the middle-aged guy who drank too much. And there were journalists who were just itching to take him on, especially Edward R. Murrow on his documentary TV show *See It Now*.

FRED FRIENDLY, PRODUCER OF *SEE IT NOW*: I can still recall Murrow's impish grin as he thrust a *Detroit News* article my way.

MURROW: Fritzl, this could be the little picture for your McCarthy story.

FRIENDLY: He was one of the select few who could get away with calling me that. "My McCarthy story," as he put it, referred to a question that was being asked of us almost daily that fall of 1953: when would Ed Murrow take on Joe McCarthy? Ed and I had discussed the matter in private many times. We agreed that when we did move there could be no margin for error, our story had to be directly on point.

FLY ON THE WALL: The story was about Air Force reservist Milo Radulovich, the son of a Serbian immigrant, who had been with the service for ten years. With no warning, the lieutenant was asked to resign. When he asked why, he was told that it was because his father and sister were suspected of being communists, even though his own loyalty was unquestioned. He refused to resign; a board heard his case and recommended he be discharged anyway.

> **EDWARD R. MURROW (*SEE IT NOW*, OCTOBER 20,**
> **1953):** Good evening. A few weeks ago, there occurred a few obscure notices in the newspaper about Milo Radulovich.

FLY ON THE WALL: Radulovich's father was from Serbia, and he had subscribed to several Serbian newspapers, including one that was communist backed. His sister had made donations to support Paul Robeson.

> **MURROW:** This is his sister, Margaret Radulovich Fishman. She neither defends nor explains her political activities.

> **FISHMAN:** I feel that my activities, be what they may—my political beliefs are my own private affair . . . Since when can a man be adjudged guilty, which is in effect what's happened

to him, because of the alleged political beliefs or activities of a member of his family.

FLY ON THE WALL: Milo Radulovich was told that he could avoid discharge if he publicly denounced his father and sister.

> **RADULOVICH:** I am his son and I am her brother, and I certainly can't cut the blood tie nor do I wish to . . . The word "denounced" . . . means saying something to punish an individual and so actually attacking the individual himself.

> **JOE WERSHBA, *SEE IT NOW* REPORTER:** What happens to your two children—your five-year-old and five-month-old—in terms of you?

> **RADULOVICH:** If I am being judged on my relatives, are my children going to be asked to denounce me? Are they going to be judged on what their father was labeled? Are they going to have to explain to their friends, et cetera, why their father's a security risk?

> **WERSHBA:** Just what is your view of democracy?

> **RADULOVICH:** Well, I believe that democracy is a state of being where the society is free. Each individual is free to do as he chooses, as long as it does not bring physical harm, or physical danger or impoverishment, or anything like that, to other individuals.

FLY ON THE WALL: Murrow didn't mention McCarthy by name on *See It Now*, but he didn't have to. McCarthy himself was the master of smearing people by rumor without ever quite naming them. McCarthy sent one of his investigators to talk to Joe Wershba, the *See It Now* reporter.

> **DON SURINE:** What would you say if I told you that Murrow was on the Soviet payroll in 1934? . . . I'm not saying

that Murrow is a Commie himself, but he's one of those goddamn anti-anti-Communists, and they're just as dangerous. And let's face it. If it walks like a duck, talks like a duck, and acts like a duck, then, goddamn, it is a duck!

FLY ON THE WALL: When Murrow heard about McCarthy's threat, it made him even more determined to gather clips for another TV show that would take on McCarthy.

SPIES IN NEW JERSEY

FLY ON THE WALL: When they were attacked, McCarthy and Roy Cohn's instincts were to shift the focus and hit back harder. They always were looking for headlines to take back the spotlight. They found the perfect target in Fort Monmouth, New Jersey. The U.S. Army Signal Corps there controlled most of the Army's communications; it employed thirty thousand scientists and engineers. Many of them were Jews from New York City, some of whom had joined progressive causes in their youth. Julius Rosenberg once worked there, and McCarthy and Cohn knew the name Rosenberg would guarantee headlines.

NEW YORK TIMES: Rosenberg Called Radar Spy Leader: McCarthy Says Ring He Set Up 'May Still Be in Operation' at Monmouth Laboratory.

ROBIN BADY, DAUGHTER OF MONMOUTH SCIENTIST: I was eight and I loved Nancy Drew—even though I didn't

look anything like her. I thought I'd be a great FBI agent. I
believed in strict law and order. It was something I got from
my father . . . that we do what was right. I went to the library
and found the address of the FBI. I sent Hoover a poem about
law and order. He wrote me: "It's wonderful that you believe
in law and order—and that you practice that respect by being
in the safety patrol. I get lots of letters—and you are the only
one who wrote a poem."

Hoover wrote me that only men can be an FBI agent.

And he sent me a lot of pamphlets about what a woman can be. "You can be a clerk or a secretary." I was disappointed.

FLY ON THE WALL: Robin Bady's father was taken off super-secret projects, but not fired. The Army felt it was doing things the correct way and wanted to get McCarthy to back off. But McCarthy wouldn't. Behind closed doors, McCarthy's subcommittee was busy questioning former and current employees of Fort Monmouth, who hadn't been named publicly. After most sessions, he would talk to the press, hinting there was a Soviet spy ring.

McCARTHY: It has all the earmarks of extremely dangerous espionage. If it develops as it has been, it will envelop the whole signal corps . . . Judging from the testimony given . . . it is indicated that some of the witnesses had associated with Rosenberg.

FLY ON THE WALL: The truth was that McCarthy's information was very sketchy. But that had never stopped McCarthy. Under the Army's investigation, dozens of scientists were suspended, not fired, including Robin's father. Robin Bady remembers how it felt when her father stopped going to work.

ROBIN BADY: There were no screams in my house. I just remember the feeling of being scared. My mother took to her bed. I knew there was something—but it was always secret . . . There were words that floated around the house—suspension and declassification—I knew they were dangerous. I didn't know why people were whispering them.

FLY ON THE WALL: Although the Army had found zero evidence to support the suspensions of the accused scientists, including Robin Bady's father, McCarthy wouldn't let it go. McCarthy hauled in General Miles Reber, who had been in charge of the investigation, and demanded to know the names of the investigators. In other words, he wanted the general to name names.

> **REBER (READING TRUMAN'S PRESIDENTIAL DIRECTIVE OF 1948):** No information shall be supplied as to any specific intermediate steps, proceedings, transcripts of hearings, or actions taken in processing individuals under loyalty or security programs.

> **McCARTHY:** Do you think we should or should not have the names of those who cleared Communists?

> **REBER:** May I say as sincerely and honestly as I can that the Department of the Army, under directions of the Secretary and the Chief of Staff, is doing everything in its power to eliminate any possibility for communism infiltrating into the Army.

> **McCARTHY:** Your general statement that you are doing everything you can to remove Communists does not mean too much.

> **DAVID OSHINSKY, HISTORIAN:** Despite his thin material, or perhaps because of it, the chairman worked up a terrific head of steam. He was "shocked beyond

words" by the Army's failure to discharge these workers. It was "the most unusual, the most unbelievable, the most unexplainable situation" he had ever come across.

FLY ON THE WALL: This was an early skirmish of the war between the U.S. Army and McCarthy. It is not so hard to make actors and writers name names, but the military has its own honor code and its own proud history. And the president of the United States was a general who had devoted his whole life to the military. The Army, like Eisenhower, wanted to avoid a major confrontation. To placate McCarthy, Secretary of the Army Robert Stevens offered the senator a private tour of the secret equipment in Fort Monmouth. Unfortunately, no one but the senator was allowed in, and Roy Cohn had to wait outside. Nobody slams the door on Roy Cohn. At least that's what Roy Cohn thought.

> **COHN:** This is war! We'll really start investigating this place now. They let communists in and keep me out!

FLY ON THE WALL: There were a lot of people that McCarthy and Cohn could push around, but in the end the Army wasn't one of them.

> **McCARTHY:** [I don't] give a tinker's dam [sic] what the bleeding hearts say . . . We are on the most important skunk hunt ever. The closer we get to the nerve center, the louder and louder will be the screams.

FLY ON THE WALL: Despite McCarthy's threats, the Army reviewed the cases and realized that all the scientists who had been accused were innocent. Robin Bady's father got his job back.

ROBIN BADY: Even though my father got his job back, there was a sense of shame that kind of enveloped my family . . . I never got over it.

COHN GOES TOO FAR, AND THE WHITE HOUSE SETS A TRAP

FLY ON THE WALL: As far as Roy Cohn was concerned, the Fort Monmouth investigation was a huge success for McCarthy. McCarthy was back in the spotlight. But Cohn had his own problem. Every male citizen between the ages of eighteen and twenty-six had to register for the draft and, if called, had to serve in the military. In November 1953, Cohn's protégé and European tour companion, David Schine, was drafted. Cohn had tried to get him into the Army reserves as an officer and be assigned to McCarthy's committee.

TOM WOLFE, BOOK REVIEWER: David Schine had been classified 4-F because of a slipped disk, but now the highly publicized, hard-partying lad was re-examined and reclassified 1-A.

GENERAL MILES REBER: I received numerous telephone calls from Mr. Cohn urging speed in this case . . . At times I received two and three telephone calls a day. . . . I recall no instance under which I was put under greater pressure.

WOLFE: Cohn made calls to everyone from Secretary of the Army Robert Stevens on down. He made small talk, he made big talk, he tried to make deals, he tendered i.o.u.'s, he screamed, and he screamed some more, he spoke of grim consequences.

FLY ON THE WALL: Cohn had tried to humiliate him in the Monmouth hearings. To make things worse, the year before, General Reber's brother had been forced out of the State Department because of rumors that his brother was a homosexual. So, despite Cohn's efforts, Schine went into the Army as a private. Even Elvis Presley, much more famous than David Schine, had to go into the Army as a private.

COHN: The Army is making Dave eat shit because he works for Joe.

FLY ON THE WALL: After Schine began basic training, Cohn helped him get weekend and weekday evening passes and tried to have him reassigned back to McCarthy's committee. McCarthy's political instincts were still working. He knew that Cohn's demand for favors for David Schine was a political land mine. He called Robert Stevens, the secretary of the Army.

McCARTHY: I would like to ask you one personal favor. For God's sake, don't put Dave in Service and assign him back to my committee . . . He is a good boy, but there is nothing indispensable about him . . . If he could get off week-ends— Roy—it is one of the few things I have seen him completely unreasonable about. He thinks Dave should be a general and work from the penthouse of the Waldorf.

FLY ON THE WALL: The Army got tired of Cohn's relentless demands for special treatment of David Schine. John Adams, the Army's liaison with McCarthy's subcommittee, finally confronted McCarthy, who promised to get his staff to back off. Furious, Cohn called Adams two hours later.

> **COHN:** I'll teach you and I'll teach the Army what it means to go over my head.
>
> **ADAMS:** Is that a threat?

COHN: No, that's not a threat; that's a promise.

FLY ON THE WALL: The idea of special treatment for David Schine infuriated the generals, and Eisenhower was nothing if not a general. And a general who was really good at advance planning of secret attacks. After all, he had planned D-Day.

WHITE HOUSE STAFF MEMO, "RESPONDING TO SENATOR McCARTHY":

I. Main Points for Consideration

   A. Senator McCarthy has attacked the President, and the President's prestige is threatened both in this country and abroad.

   B. Would a response by the President add dignity and status to the attack?

   C. Will a response to McCarthy jeopardize the legislative program?

McCARTHY HUNTS FOR COMMIES
AND BAGS A DENTIST

FLY ON THE WALL: Eisenhower surrounded himself with not just military advisers, but a staff with sharp political instincts who saw their job as guarding the prestige of the presidency. Eisenhower understood that the United States was now a dominant power in what was hardening as the Cold War. He was much more focused on that, and he didn't waste any more time than necessary on McCarthy. On December 8, 1953, Eisenhower gave a visionary speech to the United Nations.

EISENHOWER: The dread secret, and the fearful engines of atomic might, are not ours alone . . . So my country's purpose is to help us move out of the dark chamber of horrors into the light . . . The United States would seek more than the mere reduction or elimination of atomic materials for military purposes. It is not enough to take this weapon out of the hands of soldiers . . . This greatest of destructive powers can be developed into a great boon, for the benefit of all mankind. The United States knows that peaceful power from atomic energy is no dream of the future. That capability, already proved, is here—now—today.

WILLIAM S. WHITE, *NEW YORK TIMES* REPORTER:
President Eisenhower's overture to the Russians to accept peaceful internationalization of atomic power has greatly strengthened his hand in world affairs and against critics in his own party.

FLY ON THE WALL: McCarthy was not going to sit on the sidelines while Eisenhower got the headlines. As usual, Cohn thought he had the solution. He got a tip that a medical officer at Camp Kilmer in New Jersey had gone to school with Julius Rosenberg. As far as Cohn was concerned, this made the man a headline grabber and a communist. He called up the subcommittee's Army liaison, John Adams.

JOHN ADAMS: It is both typical and ironic that ultimate confrontation between the Army and Joe McCarthy was over the promotion of a dentist. The unpleasantries began, like so many others that January, with a phone call from Roy Cohn.

ROY COHN: [There's] a captain or a major, a doctor or a dentist, who is on duty at Camp Kilmer, and who is a Communist.

FLY ON THE WALL: Now a dentist might not seem like an extreme threat to American democracy, but to those commie hunters, Cohn and McCarthy, it was.

The dentist, Irving Peress, had been drafted into the Army and, like all doctors and dentists, entered as an officer. The Army had sent him the standard loyalty questionnaire, which asked whether he had

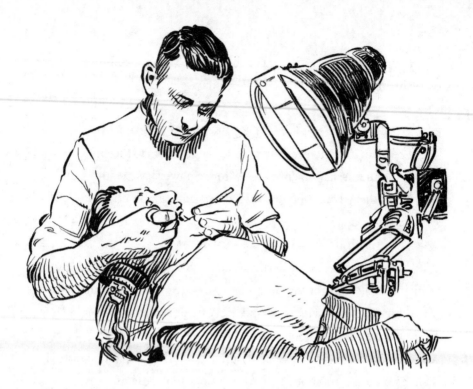

ever been a communist. But Peress didn't fill it out. He had simply written, "Federal Constitutional Privilege." Army officials didn't notice, and he was promoted, along with all doctors and dentists, several months later. When his omission was discovered, termination procedures began immediately. Peress was set to be honorably discharged in ninety days. McCarthy decided to hold hearings about it.

McCARTHY: Did anyone in the Army ever ask you whether you were a member of the Communist Party or a Communist Party organizer?

PERESS: I decline to answer that question under the protection of the Fifth Amendment on the ground that it might tend to incriminate me.

McCARTHY: Is your wife a member of the Communist Party?

PERESS: I again claim the privilege.

FLY ON THE WALL: McCarthy expected the Peress case to prove what a great communist hunter he was. But it didn't turn out to be the kind of publicity McCarthy and Cohn wanted. Instead, they were laughed at for picking on a dentist.

>**TIME MAGAZINE:** Senator Joe McCarthy, after a fortnight of mounting frenzy, had built the smallest of molehills into one of the most devasting political volcanoes that ever poured the lava of conflict and the ash of dismay over Washington.

FLY ON THE WALL: The general in charge of Camp Kilmer, where Peress was stationed, was General Ralph W. Zwicker, a World War II hero who had commanded a regiment in the deadly Battle of the Bulge and had won many honors for his bravery. That didn't matter to McCarthy and Cohn, who hauled General Zwicker before their committee and asked him about Peress.

>**McCARTHY:** Did you know that he refused to answer questions about his Communist activities?
>
>**ZWICKER:** Specifically, I don't believe so.
>
>**McCARTHY:** Did you have any idea?
>
>**ZWICKER:** Of course, I had an idea.

McCARTHY: Then you knew that those were the questions he was asked, did you not? General, let's try and be truthful. I'm going to keep you here as long as you keep hedging and hemming.

ZWICKER: I'm not hedging.

McCARTHY: Or hawing.

ZWICKER: I am not hawing, and I don't like to have anyone impugn my honesty, which you just about did.

McCARTHY: Either your honesty or your intelligence; I can't help impugning one or the other. . . .

ZWICKER: I was never officially informed by anyone that he was part of a Communist conspiracy, Mr. Senator.

McCARTHY: You say insofar as the Communist conspiracy is concerned, you need an official notification?

ZWICKER: Yes, sir.

FLY ON THE WALL: McCarthy proceeded to make up a hypothetical situation in which a General Smith approved the honorable discharge of an officer who, like Peress, took the Fifth when asked whether he was a member of the Communist Party.

McCARTHY: Do you think that General Smith should be removed from the military?

FLY ON THE WALL: The general hesitated, not quite grasping what he was being asked. McCarthy had the question reread twice and badgered him into answering.

ZWICKER: I do not think he should be removed from the military.

McCARTHY: Then General, you should be removed from any command. Any man who has been given the honor of being promoted to general and who says, "I will protect another general who protected Communists," is not fit to wear that uniform, General . . . You think it is proper to give an honorable discharge to a man who is known to be a Communist?

FLY ON THE WALL: Eisenhower was furious that McCarthy would treat one of his generals like that. Beyond what Eisenhower thought about McCarthy, he believed that an attack on the dignity and honor of the Army could not stand, and he had a loyal staff to help figure out a strategy to bring McCarthy down, once and for all.

SHERMAN ADAMS, EISENHOWER'S CHIEF OF STAFF: Have you a record of this?

JOHN ADAMS, ARMY COUNSEL: I do not.

SHERMAN ADAMS: Don't you think you ought to start one?

FLY ON THE WALL: John Adams, the Army's liaison with the McCarthy subcommittee, set to work compiling a thirty-four-page document on the Army's dealings with McCarthy and Cohn. It would eventually be called the *Chronology of Events*, but around the Pentagon, the document was known as the "atomic weapon."

THE NOOSE AROUND
McCARTHY'S NECK GETS TIGHTER

FLY ON THE WALL: Eisenhower wasn't quite ready to give McCarthy more publicity by taking him on publicly. First, he tried one last time to negotiate with McCarthy to stop antagonizing his Army. Secretary of the Army Robert Stevens met with McCarthy and other leading Republican senators.

> **DAVID OSHINSKY:** The luncheon meeting was supposed to be "super-secret" . . . Over a luncheon table that included fried chicken, salad and coffee, the senators went at Stevens like a police interrogation team.

FLY ON THE WALL: This became a famous chicken lunch, with the emphasis on the chicken. They were trying to negotiate how the Army would complete the Peress investigation quickly and quietly. But McCarthy ambushed the process by dishing to the press.

> **McCARTHY:** Stevens couldn't have conceded more if he crawled in on his hands and knees.

FLY ON THE WALL: McCarthy wanted to make it seem that Stevens and the Army were more interested in defending themselves than chasing communists. But he didn't get the press he was expecting.

> **RICHMOND NEWS LEADER, VIRGINIA:** By supinely capitulating, Mr. Stevens has merely heightened political tensions, and contributed to the delusion that McCarthy bestrides this nation like some Colossus, while petty men walk around under his huge legs.

> **CHICAGO TRIBUNE:** It seems to us that Sen. McCarthy will better serve his cause if he learns to distinguish the role of investigator from the role of avenging angel.

> **MILWAUKEE JOURNAL:** Secretary of the Army Stevens denies that he retreated before McCarthy. If it was not retreat, it was total collapse . . . It is time for President Eisenhower to step into this expanding battle of McCarthy against the United States government.

FLY ON THE WALL: Eisenhower's closest associates agreed that it was time for the president to take on McCarthy directly. Henry Cabot Lodge, Eisenhower's former campaign manager, warned the president of McCarthy's motives.

> **LODGE:** Investigation of the Army, while ostensibly aimed at making sure that the Army is secure against communist penetration, is actually a part of an attempt to destroy you politically.

The president tried to rally his troops.

VICE PRESIDENT RICHARD NIXON: The President seems to have been convinced that people in the administration were actually afraid of McCarthy . . . He wanted to see smiling faces around him.

EISENHOWER (TO REPUBLICAN CONGRESSIONAL LEADERS): Let's go out and grin at the world. It's about time we developed a sense of humor.

JAMES HAGERTY, WHITE HOUSE PRESS SECRETARY (IN DIARY, MARCH 8, 1954): I talked to Pres. in gym— as he was changing clothes to go out on lawn to hit golf balls—it was agreed that I should sort of leak story on McCarthy action tomorrow.

NICHOLAS VON HOFFMAN, ROY COHN'S BIOGRAPHER: That the weapon would soon be coming was the best unkept secret in the city.

FLY ON THE WALL: Columnist Joseph Alsop dropped by Army counsel John Adams's office for a chat. He wanted to know what was going on with the Army's conflict with McCarthy. Adams reached into a drawer.

ADAMS: It would be quicker and more accurate if you just read this.

FLY ON THE WALL: Adams handed Alsop his memorandum on McCarthy and Cohn's abuses, saying the information was off the record. Alsop couldn't print a word about it or its contents.

ADAMS: He agreed and began reading, snickering from time to time.

FLY ON THE WALL: On March 3, President Eisenhower held a press conference. Reporters were drooling over all the leaks around town, and they expected Eisenhower to really get his teeth into McCarthy.

EISENHOWER: In opposing communism, we are defeating ourselves if either by design or through carelessness we use methods that do not conform to the American sense of justice and fair play.

FLY ON THE WALL: The reporters were looking for something that would make headlines, and this wasn't it. Yet again, Eisenhower never mentioned McCarthy by name.

JOSEPH ALSOP (YELLING): Why, the yellow son of a bitch!

FLY ON THE WALL: McCarthy wasn't fooled. He got that Eisenhower was gunning for him and that the leaks were largely coming from the White House. McCarthy called the reporters so he could make his own headlines.

McCARTHY: If a stupid, arrogant or witless man in a position of power appears before our committee and is found aiding the Communist Party, he will be exposed.

JAMES RESTON, JOURNALIST: President Eisenhower turned the other cheek today, and Senator Joseph R. McCarthy, always an obliging fellow, struck him about as hard as the position of the President will allow.

FLY ON THE WALL: Adlai Stevenson, the Democrat who lost to Eisenhower in 1952, gave the speech that everyone had expected Eisenhower to make. But Eisenhower was a strategist. He preferred that the public attack on McCarthy come from Democrats, rather than openly from a Republican.

> **STEVENSON:** Extremism produces extremism, lies beget lies . . . When demagoguery and deceit become a national political movement, we Americans are in trouble . . . A group of political plungers has persuaded the President that McCarthyism is the best Republican formula for political success.

> **NEW YORK TIMES:** STEVENSON SAYS PRESIDENT YIELDS TO 'M'CARTHYISM'

FLY ON THE WALL: McCarthy went to the television networks without asking the White House and told them he would give the Republican response to Stevenson. Eisenhower said he would not.

> **EISENHOWER, AS RECALLED BY NIXON:** I think we probably ought to use Dick more than we have been. He can sometimes take positions which are more political than it would be expected that I take. The difficulty with the McCarthy problem is that anybody who takes it on runs the risk of being called a pink. Dick has had experience in the communist field, and therefore he would not be subject to criticism.

FLY ON THE WALL: The vice president was a good choice.

NIXON (IN TELEVISED SPEECH, MARCH 13, 1954):
When you go out and shoot rats, you have to shoot straight, because when you shoot wildly, it not only means that the rats may get away more easily—but you make it easier on the rats. Also you might hit someone else who is trying to shoot rats, too. So, we have to be fair—for two very good reasons: one, because it is right; and two, because it is the most effective way of doing the job.

FLY ON THE WALL: Senator McCarthy knew he was the rat.

McCARTHY: That prick Nixon, kissing Ike's ass to make it to the White House.

FLY ON THE WALL: Meanwhile, Eisenhower was moving according to his plan. He had his chief of staff invite Senator Ralph Flanders to the White House. The next day on the Senate floor, Flanders made the most exciting speech of his career. Up until then . . . the Republican from Vermont had never made news.

DAVID OSHINSKY: The word "invisible" probably described him best.

FLANDERS: This brief talk is in the nature of advice to the junior senator of Wisconsin . . . He found dirt under the rug . . . All this dirt he found and displayed . . . Of course it was not done quietly . . . Perhaps these extremes are necessary if a one-man party is to be kept in the headlines and in the limelight . . . In very truth, the world seems to be mobilizing for the great battle of Armageddon. Now is a crisis in the agelong warfare between God and the Devil for the souls of men. In this battle of the agelong war, what is the part played by the junior senator from Wisconsin? He dons his war paint. He goes into his war dance. He emits his war whoops. He goes forth to battle and proudly returns with the scalp of a pink Army dentist.

EISENHOWER (IN LETTER TO FLANDERS): I think America needs to hear more Republican voices like yours.

JOE McCARTHY AND HIS TERRIBLE, HORRIBLE, NO GOOD, VERY BAD WEEK

FLY ON THE WALL: On the same day that Flanders made his speech, there was a large ad next to the radio and television listings in the *New York Times*.

> **ADVERTISEMENT:** Tonight at 10:30, SEE IT NOW, a report on Senator Joseph R. McCarthy.

> **EDWARD R. MURROW (PRIVATELY):** You know, the man to destroy this guy is Mr. Joe himself.

> **WALT KELLY, CREATOR OF POGO COMIC STRIP:** Will he take the job?

FLY ON THE WALL: Murrow and Fred Friendly decided it was time to take on McCarthy directly. Their team had gone through fifteen thousand feet of film of McCarthy, realizing that most people, even his

supporters, had never really seen him in action. Murrow started the show in the voice that America loved.

HOWARD K. SMITH, ANOTHER BROADCASTER: Ed could say "twenty-six" and it sounded like the most important declaration ever made by man.

MURROW: Good evening. Tonight *See It Now* devotes its entire half hour to a report on Senator Joseph R. McCarthy, told mainly in his own words and pictures.

FLY ON THE WALL: The clips that Murrow showed were not flattering.

JOSEPH E. PERSICO, HISTORIAN: There was the high-pitched giggle, ridiculous yet frightening, even a little mad.

NEIL McDONALD, HISTORIAN: Murrow plays a sound tape of the senator's notorious accusation of twenty years of "Democratic treason" and "historic betrayal." A series of clips follow providing background . . . One shows McCarthy's nervous giggle, where he seems not quite sane.

MURROW: We must remember always that accusation is not proof and that conviction depends upon evidence and due process of law. We will not walk in fear, one of another . . . This is no time for men who oppose Senator McCarthy's methods to keep silent . . . We proclaim ourselves, as indeed we are, the defenders of freedom, wherever it continues to exist in the world, but we cannot defend freedom abroad by deserting it at home . . . Good night, and good luck.

FLY ON THE WALL: Within forty-eight hours CBS had received more than twelve thousand phone calls. Callers who liked the show outnumbered the ones who didn't ten to one. But there was still plenty of hate mail. One suggested an inscription for a new Murrow-style Statue of Liberty.

LETTER FROM VIEWER: Send me your Commies, pinkos, and crackpots, and I will put them on television.

FLY ON THE WALL: Despite the mostly positive response at CBS, across the country, polls showed that 64 percent of the American people still had no problem with the way Joe McCarthy was fighting communism. But that was before the White House made public their not-so-secret bombshell.

JAMES HAGERTY, WHITE HOUSE PRESS SECRETARY (IN DIARY, MARCH 11): Army report on Schine-Cohn-McCarthy going up on Hill today—it's a pip—shows constant pressure by Cohn to get Schine soft Army job, with Joe in and out of threats . . . Should bust things wide open.

FLY ON THE WALL: Up until that day, Congress had not seen the official report about Cohn demanding special favors for Schine. Senator Charles Potter, a Republican member of McCarthy's Senate subcommittee, stormed into McCarthy's office.

POTTER: Cohn has to go. We've got to get rid of him.

McCARTHY: It's blackmail, Potter . . . It's a fraud. If I get rid of Roy it would be the greatest victory the Communists have scored up to now. He's indispensable.

FLY ON THE WALL: McCarthy couldn't see how vulnerable Cohn was making him.

MICHAEL STRAIGHT, JOURNALIST: Master though he was, McCarthy without Cohn was only half a man.

FLY ON THE WALL: Editors across the country delayed the morning edition to get out the story that Roy Cohn, McCarthy's right-hand man, had tried to get special treatment for David Schine.

UNITED PRESS: The Army charged in a sensational report that Sen. Joseph R. McCarthy used pressure . . . to get soft treatment for a drafted McCarthy investigator . . . The Army's dynamite-laden document . . . [landed] like a bombshell in the middle of the McCarthy controversy.

JACK ANDERSON, INVESTIGATIVE REPORTER FOR COLUMNIST DREW PEARSON: At last McCarthy had been caught in the one offense that is indefensible in a society that runs on egalitarian rhetoric—the use of political pull to excuse a millionaire's boy from peeling the potatoes that other mothers' sons had to peel.

ROY COHN PUNCHES BACK

FLY ON THE WALL: McCarthy had never expected that Cohn and Schine's antics could put him in so much jeopardy. He tried to change the subject.

> **McCARTHY:** I don't answer charges; I make them.

> **NEW YORK TIMES:** Senator Joseph McCarthy declared tonight that he did not "give a tinker's damn" about criticism about his red-hunting "methods," no matter "how high or how low" were critics in either political party . . . He said that he had not started the controversy with the Eisenhower administration, "but I think that maybe I will have to finish it."

FLY ON THE WALL: Roy Cohn and McCarthy knew that in order to fight back they were going to have to try to produce documents that refuted the charges that they had tried to get Schine special treatment. McCarthy's staff pulled an all-nighter. In the morning, they miraculously were able to produce eleven memos that, oddly enough, fit exactly the dates of the Army's reports but were completely different.

> **COHN:** Instead of our pressuring the Army on behalf of Dave Schine, the Army was trying to do everything to silence us. And we had the documentation.

> **NEW YORK TIMES:** Senator Joseph R. McCarthy today angrily charged the Army with attempted blackmail in an effort to stop his exposure of Communists.

> **COHN:** No improper influence was ever exerted by me. . . . I didn't say I would wreck the Army. I never threatened anyone or did any other such absurd thing.

FLY ON THE WALL: The Pentagon, Secretary of the Army Robert Stevens, and even President Eisenhower were stunned to hear that *they* were the ones who were blackmailing McCarthy.

> **STEVENS:** Utterly untrue. Anyone who knows me would realize that such a charge is fantastic.

> **JOHN ADAMS, ARMY COUNSEL:** Fantastic and false.

> **JAMES HAGERTY, PRESS SECRETARY (IN DIARY, MAY 12):** President getting pretty sick and tired of McCarthy.

> **SENATOR CHARLES POTTER:** Someone is lying, and we've got to find out who it is.

FLY ON THE WALL: The public wanted to find out who was telling the truth: McCarthy and Cohn or the Army. On the morning of March 16, 1954, McCarthy's Permanent Subcommittee on Investigations met to try to figure out what to do. Senator John L. McClellan, a Democrat from Arkansas, spoke up.

> **McCLELLAN:** It is our baby, and it is our linen, and we have got to wash it, and I favor washing it in public.

FLY ON THE WALL: Even McCarthy knew that it was too much to be the chair at his own hearing. So he agreed to step down and let Karl Mundt, the ranking Republican on the committee, take the chair. But McCarthy would be allowed to cross-examine all the witnesses.

> **NEW YORK TIMES:** This is a little like saying that Mr. McCarthy has so graciously agreed to investigate himself.

FLY ON THE WALL: The only question was whether the hearings on the Army versus McCarthy should be done in private or public. McCarthy wanted to operate the way he always did, behind closed doors as much as possible, so he could be the first person to step out and talk to the press.

> **JAMES HAGERTY (IN DIARY):** Ike wants hearings open and televised.

> **EISENHOWER:** I've made up my mind you can't do business with Joe and to hell with any attempt to compromise.

FLY ON THE WALL: The Army-McCarthy hearings were televised. McCarthy thought the Army was on trial. That was not Eisenhower's plan. He would not let McCarthy attack the Army. He was going to bring McCarthy down. And as it turned out, McCarthy was going to help him.

THE ARMY-McCARTHY HEARINGS: TELEVISION SENSATION OF THE CENTURY

FLY ON THE WALL: On Thursday morning, April 22, 1954, thirty million people switched on their televisions to watch, and another fifty million listened on the radio. People who didn't have TVs rushed out to get them. The networks stopped all soap operas to provide gavel-to-gavel coverage. Department stores noticed there were very few daytime customers, and kids, including these authors, were surprised to come home from school and see their parents glued to the TV.

MICHAEL STRAIGHT, JOURNALIST: At seven that morning the first group of spectators had gathered in the rotunda of the Senate Office Building. Three hours later, eight hundred were herded through oaken doors into the 74-foot-long room, built in 1909 to hold three hundred . . . In front of the windows had been raised four powerful floodlamps. Those who glanced up could hardly see anything else. Those who looked, squinting and blinking across the room, soon found that the sockets of their eyes were aching from the glare. So the subordination of the participants in the room to the audience beyond was at once established.

FLY ON THE WALL: At precisely 10:30 a.m., Senator Karl Mundt took his pipe out of his mouth and banged an ashtray on the table, calling the hearings to order. He had a gavel; he just preferred an ashtray. The show had begun. There were a few new characters in the cast. Each side got to choose an attorney. The subcommittee chose Ray Jenkins, a successful and flamboyant criminal lawyer from Knoxville, Tennessee. Jenkins was a steadfast Republican, but he claimed to have no opinion about McCarthy. The Army hired Joseph Welch, a trial lawyer from Boston.

DAVID OSHINSKY: The reporters . . . kept asking, "Who is that?" . . . A superb courtroom lawyer, his style—unlike Ray Jenkins's—was subtle, self-effacing, and sly.

FLY ON THE WALL: Welch invited two young lawyers from his firm to assist him in Washington.

WELCH: Boys, I don't know anything about you except I have always liked you, but if there is anything funny in the life of anyone of you that would hurt anybody in this case you speak up quick.

FRED FISHER: Mr. Welch, when I was in law school and for a period of months after, I belonged to the Lawyers Guild.

FLY ON THE WALL: The House of Un-American Activities had labeled the National Lawyers Guild as the legal arm of the Communist Party. This was serious. Welch and Fisher decided to consult Eisenhower's press secretary, Jim Hagerty. Hagerty at first said no problem.

HAGERTY: [You can] count on a friend in the White House—my boss, the President.

FLY ON THE WALL: Then Fisher mentioned he had established a guild chapter with the assistance of a well-known communist organizer.

> **HAGERTY (IN DIARY, APRIL 2):** [That] association was a different story. It was decided Fisher to drop out and go back to Boston—too dangerous to give McCarthy opportunity to brand Fisher as Red and smear up Army defense . . . tough decision, but necessary.

FLY ON THE WALL: The hearings began without Fisher on April 22. Mundt made some opening remarks, stating his expectations for behavior and outlining the reason they were all there: to decide if McCarthy and Cohn had tried to get special treatment for Schine, or whether the Army was keeping Schine a lowly private to force McCarthy's subcommittee to end its investigation of communist infiltration of the Army.

> **MUNDT:** Our counsel, Mr. Jenkins, will now call the first witness.

> **McCARTHY:** A point of order, Mr. Chairman. May I raise a point of order?

FLY ON THE WALL: It was the first of so many "points of order" that it became a national catchphrase.

> **MICHAEL STRAIGHT:** McCarthy, ill-tempered from the first, seemed to know he should never have permitted himself to be cast defending the privileges of an overly indulged son of a millionaire.

HAYNES JOHNSON, HISTORIAN: Television enabled the American people to see the real Joe McCarthy, live and unfiltered—snarling, blustering, abusing, bullying, giggling, threatening, lying, filibustering—for thirty-six days.

STRAIGHT: Each afternoon Joseph McCarthy appeared freshly shaved, his face caked with a cream-colored makeup, which from nearby gave a startling aspect to his jowls.

FLY ON THE WALL: Every day more and more people tuned in to the hearings.

WELCH: There was something about these hearings that seemed to affect the public like a habit-forming drug.

COLLIER'S MAGAZINE: It is safe to assume that more than half the people who viewed the Army-McCarthy hearings had never seen Congress in action before. If they had envisioned Congressional procedure as something marked by statesmanship, responsibility, befitting seriousness and, above all, dignity, they must have suffered a rude disillusionment . . . The hearings seemed to us as pretty much a disgrace to the tradition of a Senate where great men have served, great words have been spoken and great decisions made . . . It was a carnival. A sprawling, brawling travesty.

FLY ON THE WALL: Some Republicans who supported McCarthy made attempts to shorten the hearings, but Eisenhower wanted the hearings to keep going.

EISENHOWER: We've got the bastard exactly where we want him.

HAVE YOU NO SENSE
OF DECENCY?

FLY ON THE WALL: The public was transfixed. Finally, at long last, Roy Cohn was going to testify in person. The man who had been so important, but still somewhat invisible, was going to testify in front of the television cameras.

> **MICHAEL STRAIGHT:** He seemed rather like a cherub gone to seed: his cheeks puffed, his sensual mouth turned down at the corners.

FLY ON THE WALL: Cohn was concerned about what would come out in his testimony. As it happened, Cohn had used family connections to get a deferment during World War II. If that came out, it certainly wouldn't look very good. And now Cohn was supposed to say under oath that he had not tried to get David Schine special favors from the Army. As always, Cohn acted to protect himself. On the way out of the hearings June 7, he approached Welch.

COHN: There is something I would like to talk to you about privately.

FLY ON THE WALL: They entered an empty committee room and shut the door.

COHN: I know there have been imputations that I attempted to dodge the draft.

WELCH: If you will omit any reference to the Fisher case, I will not return to the topic you want me to stay away from.

FLY ON THE WALL: They had come to an agreement. Welch would drop the draft-dodging issue, and Cohn and McCarthy would not mention Fred Fisher, the young lawyer who had been sent back to Boston because of his past Lawyers Guild connection.

COHN: We shook hands . . . That evening, I went to Senator McCarthy's home and gave him a full account of my conversation with Welch and the agreement into which I had entered. *McCarthy approved the trade.*

FLY ON THE WALL: When Cohn finally took the stand on June 9, Welch stuck to the deal and did not bring up Cohn's deferment. But he found many ways to use sarcasm and other of Cohn's own tricks to needle him.

WELCH (TO COHN): May I add in my small voice, sir, and say whenever you know about a subversive or a

Communist or a spy, please hurry. Will you remember those words?

McCARTHY: Mr. Chairman, in view of that question—

MUNDT: Have you a point of order?

McCARTHY: Not exactly, Mr. Chairman, but in view of Mr. Welch's request that information be given once we know of anyone who might be performing any work for the Communist Party, I think we should tell him that he has in his law firm a young man named Fisher whom he recommended, incidentally . . . who has been for a number of years a member of an organization which was named, oh, years and years ago, as the legal bulwark of the Communist Party . . .

FLY ON THE WALL: Once Cohn realized what McCarthy was doing, he turned pale. McCarthy was violating the agreement. Even worse, Cohn knew that there was no stopping him now.

TIME MAGAZINE: Roy Cohn grimaced toward McCarthy, shook his head, and his lips seemed to form the words "No! No!"

COHN: I swiftly scribbled out a note and had it sent over by page. It read: "This is the subject which I have committed to Welch we would not go into. Please respect our agreement as an agreement because this is not going to do any good."

FLY ON THE WALL: But McCarthy continued.

McCARTHY: Knowing that, Mr. Welch, I just felt I had a duty to respond to your urgent request that before sundown, when we know of anyone serving the Communist cause, we let the agency know. We are now letting you know that your man did belong to this organization for either three or four years, belonged to it long after he was out of law school. I don't think you can find anyplace, anywhere, an organization which has done more . . . to defend Communists, to defend espionage agents, and to aid the Communist cause, than the man whom you originally wanted down here at your right hand.

FLY ON THE WALL: McCarthy finished his harangue, then looked down and began shuffling papers.

WELCH: Senator McCarthy . . . May I have your attention?

McCARTHY: I am listening to you. I can listen with one ear.

WELCH: This time I want you to listen with both.

FLY ON THE WALL: What Welch said next became the most famous moment in the hearings.

WELCH: Until this moment, Senator, I think I have never really gauged your cruelty or your recklessness . . . Little did I dream that you could be so reckless and cruel as to do an injury to that lad . . . I fear he shall always bear a scar needlessly inflicted by you. If it were in my power to forgive you for your reckless cruelty, I will do so. I like to think I'm

a gentleman, but your forgiveness will have to come from someone other than me.

McCARTHY: May I say that Mr. Welch talks about this being cruel and reckless. He was just baiting; he has been baiting Mr. Cohn here for hours.

FLY ON THE WALL: McCarthy tried to talk more about Fisher's record, but Welch would have none of it.

WELCH: Let us not assassinate this lad further, Senator. You have done enough. Have you no sense of decency, sir, at long last? Have you left no sense of decency?

FLY ON THE WALL: The crowd of spectators burst into applause. At the end of the session, Welch walked out of the hearing room, trailed by a herd of reporters. McCarthy was left in an empty meeting room.

McCARTHY (HANDS SPREAD, PALMS UP): What did I do?

FLY ON THE WALL: There are two famous speeches from the McCarthy era. One is McCarthy's speech in Wheeling, West Virginia, which was never saved on tape. The other was the McCarthy-Welch exchange at the Army-McCarthy hearings, and for that we have every word.

McCARTHY'S CENSURE
AND THEN HIS END

FLY ON THE WALL: McCarthy's troubles were far from over. On June 11, Senator Flanders introduced a motion to strip McCarthy of his chairmanship of the Government Operations committee.

> **McCARTHY:** I think they should get a man with a net and take him to a good quiet place.

FLY ON THE WALL: McCarthy's fellow senators appeared shocked he would say something so rude about a colleague. Roy Cohn later told a story about what happened when McCarthy asked one of his fellow Republicans what he had done.

> **SENATOR WILLIAM JENNER, REPUBLICAN FROM INDIANA:** You're the kid who came to the party and peed in the lemonade.

FLY ON THE WALL: On June 17, the Army-McCarthy hearings

recessed. On July 30, Flanders introduced a senate resolution calling for McCarthy's censure.

"Censure" means that the Senate as a formal body is criticizing a member's behavior. In its 165 years, the U.S. Senate had considered only two motions of censure. The first, in 1902, was against two senators who had started a fistfight on the Senate floor. The other, in 1929, was about money. Both times the senators *were* censured. It doesn't mean the senator is removed from office, but it is a badge of shame, which didn't work with McCarthy since he had no shame.

> **FLOYD M. RIDDICK, SENATE PARLIAMENTARIAN:** The McCarthy case had been building up for a long period of time. It wasn't something that just happened overnight. I remember distinctly that Senator Flanders of Vermont, for nearly six months or longer before he introduced his resolution, kept coming to the desk and asking me about the procedure on this detail and that . . . It wasn't a sudden thing of deciding to consider censure and the next day of starting out in that direction.

FLY ON THE WALL: To the public, it looked as if Flanders's outrage was directly related to "Have you no decency?" but it was a move that Eisenhower and the Republican leadership had been planning for a long time. McCarthy was now a problem to his own party, and they wanted to save the Republican Party and make it look as if they wanted to save America from the big, bad bully.

> **WILLIAM WHITE, COLUMNIST:** The controversy is deeply wounding the Republican party in the conflict between the

party's extreme Right on the one hand, and the Center and Left on the other.

FLY ON THE WALL: The problem was that once Senator Flanders's resolution to censure McCarthy was on the table, something had to be done about it.

SENATOR ARTHUR WATKINS, REPUBLICAN FROM UTAH: Last night I had the most dreadful dream. It seemed they had put me on that new committee they are setting up to study the censure charges against Senator McCarthy. And then—still worse—they made me the chairman of the committee. It was a real nightmare. I woke up shaking and struggling.

FLY ON THE WALL: Two days later, in broad daylight, it was no dream. Watkins and the other Republicans wanted the hearings to be quiet, dignified, and mostly short.

WATKINS: I intend to run an orderly hearing on McCarthy and permit no diversions.

STEWART ALSOP, COLUMNIST: It was funny in a sad sort of way, like an elderly mouse telling how he would keep the man-eating tiger under control.

FLY ON THE WALL: But that mouse roared.

SATURDAY EVENING POST: This was the very room which had housed the Army-McCarthy extravaganza, yet how different was the scene: Chairman Watkins was running things in a prim, dry, routine fashion, which was downright boring . . . Then a familiar rumble was heard:

McCARTHY: Mr. Chairman, Mr. Chairman!

WATKINS (SHARPLY): Just a moment, senator.

McCARTHY: Mr. Chairman! I should be entitled to know whether or not—

SATURDAY EVENING POST: Bang! It was the gavel swung by Chairman Watkins with startling violence.

WATKINS (CRISPLY): The senator is out of order.

SATURDAY EVENING POST: McCarthy tried two or three times more, but not even he could talk against the crack of that gavel and Watkins's grim-faced firmness. The chairman—with the final bang, bang—had the last word.

WATKINS: We are not going to be interrupted by these diversions and sidelines. We are going straight down the line. [Bang!]

JAMES RESTON, JOURNALIST: The only similarity between the Army-McCarthy hearings and today's McCarthy censure hearing was the junior senator from Wisconsin—and even Joe was different. . . . Like most repeat performances, this McCarthy hearing had trouble getting a full house.

FLY ON THE WALL: As the hearings began, not everyone was convinced that McCarthy wouldn't get away with it yet again.

RIDDICK, SENATE PARLIAMENTARIAN: Frankly, I think there was a division of feelings in there. I think the senators were concerned about the communistic infiltrations that were occurring in our government . . . but at the same time they also wanted to save the image of the Senate.

WILLIAM WHITE: Perhaps the most widely underestimated facet of Senator McCarthy's character is his almost infinite capacity to rebound from seeming disaster.

FLY ON THE WALL: But not this time. On December 2, 1954, the Senate voted to censure McCarthy, 67–22.

FRANCIS WILCOX, SENATE FOREIGN RELATIONS COMMITTEE CHIEF OF STAFF: This is what President Eisenhower thought should have been done earlier. McCarthy was a senator, and the Senate should have taken proper steps to punish him.

RIDDICK: After the Senate had voted to condemn him, [McCarthy] was really hurt.

WILCOX: After his news value began to deteriorate and he was taken off the front page . . . there were some television cameras at the door. He came dashing over waving a press release and saying to the news people who were there, "I have a news release I want to share with you." They just turned their backs and paid no attention to him. He stood there with the paper in his hand without any takers.

FLY ON THE WALL: Joe McCarthy always had a reputation for drink, and he appeared to drink more heavily after the censure.

RUTH WATT, CHIEF CLERK OF THE SUBCOMMITTEE ON INVESTIGATIONS: By the end of '55, about '56, he was in pretty bad shape . . . The White House was having a reception for all the senators . . . in late March [1957], and they were all invited except Joe McCarthy. McCarthy kept calling me over and saying, "Ruthy, go ask Mary Driscoll [his secretary] if I've heard from the White House yet, see if I've gotten an invitation," which I thought was kind of sad. I'd call Mary and she'd say, "You know very well he hasn't. He's not going to get any invitation to that party tonight." . . . But it was really kind of sad because he was at that point being ignored so much. Of course, I think it was of his own doing.

FLY ON THE WALL: On May 2, 1957, Senator Joseph R. McCarthy died in Bethesda Naval Hospital of alcoholic hepatitis, inflammation of his liver due to drinking too much. It was front-page news. Some newspaper editorials made him seem saintly, others not so much.

> **COURIER-JOURNAL, LOUISVILLE, KENTUCKY:** His rise to fame had the sudden, spectacular violence of a rocket splitting the night sky with unhealthy brilliance. With equal speed the glare faded and the spent stick came racing downward.

> **NEW YORK DAILY NEWS:** He was a complete patriot. He alerted the American people to the criminal Communist conspiracy to overthrow the Government of the United States. Though he made occasional mistakes, we think he was a great man.

> **ATLANTA JOURNAL:** The death of Senator Joseph R. McCarthy comes at a time when the nation has recovered the sense of proportion it lost during the national debate that once raged about the Wisconsin senator's head.

> **NEWARK STAR-LEDGER, NEW JERSEY:** If some of his enemies thought of him as a would-be dictator, those who

knew him were aware of a deep sense of humor that would not have permitted himself to accept blind adulation and the trappings of a dictatorship.

NEW YORK HERALD TRIBUNE: There was a genuine broad recognition that McCarthy's techniques were wrong—that shotgun blasts without regard for the fundamental rights of individuals in the line of fire were ineffective, unfair and constituted a massive assault on the civil liberties of the American people as a whole. . . . This awareness of the paramount importance of our civil liberties, ironically enough, may well be his most enduring legacy.

WILLIAM LOEB, PUBLISHER OF THE *MANCHESTER UNION LEADER*, NEW HAMPSHIRE: Joe McCarthy was murdered by the Communists . . . And did these murderers have some pretty good assistance! There was Senator Flanders, . . . then of course the piously hypocritical newspapers . . . Finally we come to that stinking hypocrite in the White House, who recently became so small that he asked every other senator and representative to his reception except Joe M'Carthy.

EPILOGUE:
WITCH HUNTS DIDN'T END

FLY ON THE WALL: Almost as soon as McCarthy died, there were conspiracy rumors about his death. Right-wing conspiracy theorists found a home in the John Birch Society, created in 1958 for the express purpose of carrying on McCarthy's crusade against communists. The John Birch Society soon grew to a membership of close to a hundred thousand with a $5 million annual budget. As the John Birch Society grew, so did the public revulsion at McCarthy's tactics. McCarthyism seemed out of step with modern America. America was changing in the 1950s.

> **JOSH, SON OF A COMMUNIST PARTY MEMBER:** My father could finally come back and out of hiding, but a lot of the harm to our family was already done. All I knew was that I didn't have a stable home.

FLY ON THE WALL: But some things stayed the same. One of Hoover's targets was still the civil rights movement.

WILLIAM SULLIVAN, FORMER HOOVER ASSISTANT:
He was very consistent throughout the years. He didn't vacillate any. The things he hated, he hated all his life. He hated liberalism, he hated blacks, he hated Jews—he had this great long list of hates.

FLY ON THE WALL: The March on Washington for Jobs and Freedom on August 28, 1963, inflamed all of Hoover's prejudices at once.

TAYLOR BRANCH, HISTORIAN: Hoover did not welcome a giant march for freedom by a race he had known over a

long lifetime as maids, chauffeurs, and criminal suspects, led by a preacher he loathed.

FLY ON THE WALL: The march went on peacefully with a record crowd of more than two hundred thousand. Its historic highlight was Martin Luther King Jr.'s "I Have a Dream" speech. Bowing to Hoover's wishes, William Sullivan, now head of the FBI's Domestic Intelligence Division, sent around a memo.

> **SULLIVAN:** In the light of King's powerful demagogic speech yesterday he stands head and shoulders over all other Negro leaders put together when it comes to influencing great masses of Negroes. We must mark him now, if we have not done so before, as the most dangerous Negro of the future of the nation from the standpoint of communism and national security.

FLY ON THE WALL: Even years after McCarthy's death, those accused still had no way to confront the evidence.

> **TOBY EMMER:** My parents were not Communist Party functionaries—they just felt there was a need for the struggle for justice. In April 1962, there was a morning newspaper story that named fifty people publicly as communists. The list had my mother's name on it. Our next-door neighbor, Mrs. Saskin, came rushing into the house.

> **MRS. SASKIN:** There is another Ruth Emmer, who is a communist. You have to protect yourself.

TOBY EMMER'S MOTHER: Mrs. Saskin, let's sit down and have coffee.

TOBY EMMER: [My mother] told [Mrs. Saskin] that she *was* the Ruth Emmer in the newspaper. My parents lost their jobs that day.

FLY ON THE WALL: Hoover remained in control of the FBI and fought against the civil rights movement and communists until his death in 1972. But witch hunts didn't end with him. People are still arguing about how many people were actually hurt during the Red Scare. Historians can't even agree on statistics.

GRIFFIN FARIELLO, HISTORIAN: By 1956, it was estimated that 13.5 million Americans were required to undergo some form of loyalty test or investigation as a condition of employment . . . How many Americans lost their jobs or were blacklisted as a consequence of the Red Scare? Those figures are difficult to determine. Many who were about to be fired chose to resign rather than risk adverse publicity. Others were fired on any available pretext . . . A tally of the suicides and premature deaths is equally difficult.

SHEILA SAMPTON, DAUGHTER OF COMMUNIST PARTY MEMBER: My father died of stomach cancer. I do remember anxiety—growing up in my house . . . when my father lost his job, which had been marginal anyway . . . In terms of salary in 1956 . . . nothing was ever explained to me.

ROBIN BADY: Nobody really talked—we knew but we didn't know—there was a sense of shame that kind of enveloped my family.

FLY ON THE WALL: So do witch hunts ever really end? In American politics it is still the kiss of unshakable death to call someone a communist.

JOSH: I have two legacies. One is to challenge what you don't think is fair and to be engaged, but also to be careful how it will affect your family and you.

TOBY EMMER: In 2006, my daughter started a family club to pass on what we learned in our family the hard way—that fear and hate are not a good way to proceed, and, because of a solid community, that if anything happened we would take care of each other.

FLY ON THE WALL: As Robin Hood would put it, at least as voiced by the writers who wrote the scripts after they were blacklisted:

> **WIFE OF OUTLAW IN ROBIN'S BAND:** No one trusts his neighbor.

> **OUTLAW:** That's the way they keep us under—by calling all those who oppose them, outlaws, and turning us against each other.

> **WOMAN WHO KEPT QUIET AFTER WITNESSING HER UNCLE'S MURDER:** [The killer] said he was a friend of the sheriff's, and if I told anyone what I'd seen, he'd see that I was branded as a witch and burned at the stake.

> **MINSTREL SONG:** The sheriff thought to set a trap with witchcraft and an aged hag. But in two ways good Robin let the cat out of the bag.

> **DWIGHT D. EISENHOWER, THIRTY-FOURTH PRESIDENT OF THE UNITED STATES:** Don't be afraid to go into your libraries and read every book . . . How will we defeat communism unless we know what it is, and what it teaches?

FLY ON THE WALL: Some witches are heroes, like the kids in the green feather club who fought for the right to read what they wanted.

TIME LINE

1848 Publication of *The Communist Manifesto* by Karl Marx and Friedrich Engels.

1914-1918 World War I.

1917 Communist Revolution in Russia.

1924 J. Edgar Hoover named head of the Bureau of Investigation (the agency was renamed the FBI in 1935).

1928-1939 Worldwide Depression throws millions out of work.

1931-1934 Famine in the Soviet Union kills millions. Stalin denies a problem exists and gets rid of anyone who speaks against him in "show trials."

1933 FDR inaugurated president and announces New Deal social programs to lift Americans out of poverty.

1933 Hitler becomes Chancellor of Germany despite receiving a minority of the votes in the national election.

1938 HUAC (House Un-American Activities Committee) established by Congress with power to investigate private citizens if they are suspected of being communists or fascists.

1939 World War II starts in Europe with Hitler's invasion of Poland.

1941 Hitler invades the Soviet Union: The Soviet Union joins Britain and France to defeat Hitler.

Japan bombs Pearl Harbor: United States declares war on Japan, and Germany and Italy declare war on the United States a few days later.

1945 HUAC is made a permanent committee.

Franklin Roosevelt dies.

Truman becomes president.

Germany surrenders.

United States drops atom bombs on Hiroshima and Nagasaki.

Japan surrenders.

1946 Isaac Woodard, returning Black veteran, attacked and blinded. Thurgood Marshall and NAACP take up his case.

Winston Churchill gives Iron Curtain speech in Missouri.

Joseph McCarthy runs for Senate and wins. Republicans sweep House and Senate for the first time since 1931.

1947 Executive Order 9835 created loyalty security program for Federal Employees.

Hollywood Ten Hearings: HUAC calls Hollywood producers, directors, and screenwriters to hearings.

1948 Berlin Blockade: Soviet Union blocks off West Berlin from all supplies. Truman orders airlift.

Republican and Democratic presidential conventions first televised.

Alger Hiss, a state department employee, is accused of being a communist by Whittaker Chambers.

Truman re-elected although everyone expected him to lose.

1949 Chinese Communists take over China.

Soviet Union detonates atom bomb.

1950 In Wheeling, West Virginia, Senator McCarthy waves paper claiming it has names (the number changes) of communists in the State Department).

Communist North Korea invades South Korea. United Nations orders troops in, and United States commits troops.

Senator Margaret Chase Smith denounces McCarthy in a Declaration of Conscience.

1951 Ethel and Julius Rosenberg tried for passing secrets to Soviet Union. They are convicted, and Roy Cohn, a young prosecutor, asks for and gets the death penalty.

I Love Lucy goes on the air.

See It Now, a TV news program hosted by Edward R. Morrow, debuts.

1952 Dwight D. Eisenhower elected first Republican president in 20 years.

"Bert the Turtle" teaches kids to "duck and cover" in order to survive an atomic attack.

Joseph McCarthy re-elected to Senate.

McCarthy made head of Government Operations (an obscure committee).

1953 Roy Cohn hired as chief investigator for McCarthy's committee.

Cohn persuades McCarthy to hire David Schine as an unpaid consultant.

Executive Order 10450 means that all government employees even suspected of being homosexual can be fired. Policy becomes known as the Lavender Scare.

Execution of Julius and Ethel Rosenberg.

End of Korean War.

See It Now with Edward Murrow shows how search for communists hurt real people.

McCarthy accuses Army of hiding spies in Fort Monmouth, New Jersey.

David Schine is drafted into the Army.

McCarthy goes after Army for promoting a dentist with suspected communist ties.

1954 *See It Now* does a whole program dedicated to showing McCarthy as a bully.

Eisenhower releases a full report to Congress on how Cohn tried to get Schine out of the Army.

Army-McCarthy hearings are televised and millions upon millions watch.

McCarthy repeatedly interrupts hearings by stating "POINT OF ORDER." Joseph Welch, the Army's attorney, famously asks McCarthy, "HAVE YOU NO DECENCY?"

Republicans lose their majority in Senate and McCarthy loses his committee.

McCarthy censured by Senate.

1955 Hoover ratchets up investigation of King and other civil rights leaders on the grounds that they are communist inspired.

1957 Joseph McCarthy dies of liver poisoning.

1961 January: United States severs ties with Cuba.

HUAC continues its investigation of "communist" influence across the country, holding hearings in several states.

NOTE ON SOURCES

In this book, we have made use of many kinds of interviews. Some of those were the ones we conducted with people whose parents had been victims of McCarthy's Red Scare. What was astonishing to us was how vivid their memories were of those times. We interviewed living relatives of some of the major players in this book. We also made use of a large collection of interviews and oral histories that the U.S. Senate Historical Office has made available.

The Congressional Record was also a rich source, as were the periodicals and newspapers of the times. McCarthy attracted a lot of attention and a lot of press coverage. All the quotes used in this book are cited. But we want our readers to understand that while every quotation may be accurate, it doesn't mean that the speaker told the truth. People lie. Joe McCarthy in particular. For example, the speech that first made him famous contained lies, and then conveniently, he lost the speech, and continued to change the numbers and facts almost daily.

The material on the Red Scare and the Cold War is vast. The documents are available in a wide variety of locations online, and particularly, the Senate Historical Office. For students who are using this book as a way to research the Red Scare, our sources will lead you to other archival material; some are easier to navigate than others. We encourage our readers who are interested in history to interview members of their own families and community to find out for themselves how this historical event might have impacted people they know. We want to emphasize that historical witch hunts affected regular people like the ones you know.

SOURCE NOTES

INTRODUCTION

xi "Robin Hood robbed the rich": United Press, "Indiana Censor Fears Little Red Robin Hood," *New York Times*, November 14, 1953.

xii "The ordeal of the swimming test": Veena Patel, "Sink or Swim: The Swimming Test in English Witchcraft," *Epoch*, August 31, 2022, epoch-magazine.com/post /sink-or-swim-the-swimming-test-in-english-witchcraft.

xii "Let the ruling classes tremble" and "Workingmen": Karl Marx and Friedrich Engels, *The Communist Manifesto*, trans. Samuel Moore (New York: Pocket Books, 1988), 116.

xiii "a ship of stone with sails of lead": "Will Form Here to Combat Reds," *Sandusky* (OH) *Star-Journal*, December 3, 1919, quoted in Morgan, *Reds*, 63.

xiv "The old world writhed": Karl Marx, *The Paris Commune*. Originally published with an introduction by Friedrich Engels, 1902. Published by New York Labor News Company, Harvard University digitalized version, June 23, 2005, 80.

xiv "The flag": "The National Flag of the RSFSR Established," Boris Yelstin Presidential Library, prlib.ru/en/history/619167.

xiv "How does one prove": Verner Clapp, Daily Reports, Chief Assistant Librarian, August 27, 1948, vol. 3, Record Group 538, Library of Congress Archives, quoted in Louise S. Robbins, "The Library of Congress and Federal Loyalty Programs, 1947– 1956: 'No Communists or . . . ,'" *Library Quarterly: Information, Community, Policy* 64, no. 4 (October 1994), 370–71.

THE DEPRESSION, FASCISM, AND THE SPECIAL COMMITTEE ON UN-AMERICAN ACTIVITIES

1 "The serfs are getting" and "They are beginning": "The Ordeal," *The Adventures of Robin Hood*, Series 1, Episode 11, screenplay by Ring Lardner Jr. (writing as Eric Heath), 1955, dailymotion.com/video/x3djk5r.

2 "My father was somebody": Sheila Sampton, interview with authors, April 30, 2018.

2 "We're never alone": "A Guest for the Gallows," *The Adventures of Robin Hood*, Series 1, Episode 12, screenplay by Ring Lardner Jr. (writing as Eric Heath), 1955, dailymotion.com/video/x6huiyf.

3 "My father started in the 1930s": Josh [last name withheld per subject's request], interview with authors, July 18, 2018.

3 "I saw what the Depression was doing": U.S. Atomic Energy Commission, *In the Matter of J. Robert Oppenheimer: Transcript of Hearing before Personnel Security Board and Texts of Principal Documents and Letters* (Cambridge, MA: MIT Press, 1954), 8, quoted in Sheinkin, *Bomb*, 11.

3 "There is no bread": *"Tell Them We Are Starving": The 1933 Soviet Diaries of Gareth Jones* (Kingston, ON: Kashtan Press, 2015), 131, quoted in Anne Applebaum, "How Stalin Hid Ukraine's Famine from the World," *Atlantic*, October 13, 2017.

3 "Living has become better": Andrew Higgins, "The Art of the Lie? The Bigger the Better," *New York Times*, January 10, 2021.

4 "This committee is determined": *Investigations of Un-American Propaganda Activities in the United States: Hearings before a Special Committee on Un-American Activities*, 75th Cong. 2 (1938) (opening statement of Chair Martin Dies).

DESTROYER OF WORLDS

5 "Scientists in Russia, Germany, England": David Munns, interview with authors, January 3, 2020.

6 "President Roosevelt Is Dead": Arthur Krock, "President Roosevelt Is Dead," *New York Times*, April 12, 1945.

6 "Last Words: 'I Have a Terrific Headache'": Associated Press, "Last Words: 'I Have a Terrific Headache,'" *New York Times*, April 12, 1945.

6 "Boys, if you ever pray": Harry S. Truman, *Memoirs*, vol. 1, *Year of Decisions* (Garden City, NY: Doubleday, 1955), 19, quoted in David McCullough, *Truman* (New York: Simon & Schuster, 1992), 353.

6 "There was an enormous flash of light": I. I. Rabi, *Science: The Center of Culture* (New York: World, 1970), 139, quoted in Sheinkin, *Bomb*, 182.

7 "We have discovered the most terrible bomb": Diary entry, July 25, 1945, in *Off*

the Record: The Private Papers of Harry S. Truman (New York: Harper & Row, 1980), 55, quoted in Sheinkin, Bomb,187.

7 "I couldn't worry about what history would say": Where the Buck Stops: The Personal and Private Writings of Harry S. Truman, ed. Margaret Truman (New York: Warner Books, 1989), 206, quoted in Sheinkin, Bomb, 189.

8 "We turned back to look at Hiroshima": Paul W. Tibbets, "How to Drop an Atom Bomb," with Wesley Price, Saturday Evening Post, June 8, 1946, 136.

9 "I had the feeling that all the human beings": Arata Osada, comp., Children of the A-Bomb: Testament of the Boys and Girls of Hiroshima (Ann Arbor, MI: Midwest Publishers, International, 1982), 237, quoted in Richard Rhodes, The Making of the Atomic Bomb, 25th anniversary ed. (New York: Simon & Schuster, 2012), 710.

9 "We knew the world would not be the same": Len Giovannitti and Fred Freed, The Decision to Drop the Bomb (New York: Coward-McCann, 1965), 197, quoted in Rhodes, Making of Atom Bomb, 676.

9 "The blood is on my hands": David McCullough, Truman (New York: Simon & Schuster, 1992), 475.

THE AMERICAN DREAM—WHOOPS, NOT SO FAST

10 "Russia will emerge from the present conflict": Office of Strategic Services, "Problems and Objectives of United States Policy," memo to president, April 2, 1945, quoted in McCullough, Truman, 372.

11 "From Stettin in the Baltic": Winston Churchill, "Sinews of Peace," speech, Westminster College, March 5, 1946, Fulton, MO, America's National Churchill Museum, nationalchurchillmuseum.org/sinews-of-peace-iron-curtain-speech.html.

12 "Flushed with their success": Library of Congress, "The Post War United States, 1945–1968: Overview," U.S. History Primary Source Timeline, loc.gov /classroom-materials/united-states-history-primary-source-timeline/post-war -united-states-1945–1968/overview/.

13 "No man who owns his own house": Eric Larrabee, "The Six Thousand Houses That Levitt Built," Harper's Magazine, September 1948, p. 84.

13 "Premises [cannot] be used or occupied": David Kushner, Levittown: Two Families, One Tycoon, and the Fight for Civil Rights in America's Legendary Suburb (New York: Walker, 2009), 43.

13 "The plain fact is": Allen Ward, "Levittown, PA: Negroes Not Wanted," *Bucks County Traveler*, June 1954, 27–28, quoted in Kushner, *Levittown*, 75.

14 "the feeling of rejection on that long ride": Bruce Lambert, "At 50, Levittown Contends with Its Legacy of Bias," *New York Times*, December 28, 1997.

14 "I came out of the service": Harry Belafonte in *Scandalize My Name: Stories from the Black List*, documentary written and directed by Alexandra M. Isles, 3DD Entertainment, 1998.

14 "My father had risked his life": Wade Hudson, *Defiant: Growing Up in the Jim Crow South* (New York: Crown, 2021), 27.

14 "Hell, no" and "God damn it, talk to me": Isaac Woodard testimony, trial transcript of *Isaac Woodard Jr. v. Atlantic Greyhound Bus Company*, Circuit Court, Kanawha County, WV, November 10–13, 1947, in Isaac Woodard Files, NAACP Papers, Library of Congress, faculty.uscupstate.edu/amyers/woodtestimony2.html.

15 "This soldier has been making": Woodard testimony, November 1947.

15 "He asked me was I discharged": Isaac Woodard Jr. affidavit, April 23, 1946, in Isaac Woodard Files, NAACP Papers, Library of Congress, faculty.uscupstate .edu/amyers/deposition.html.

15 "He told me they poured whiskey": Transcript of "The Blinding of Isaac Woodard," *American Experience*, aired March 30, 2021, on PBS, pbs.org/wgbh /americanexperience/films/blinding-isaac-woodard/#transcript.

16 "Woodard's blinding was": Olivia B. Waxman, "How a 1946 Case of Police Brutality Against a Black WWII Veteran Shaped the Fight for Civil Rights," *Time*, March 30, 2021.

16 "Hundreds of Black veterans": DeNeen L. Brown, "A Black WWII Veteran Was Beaten and Blinded, Fueling the Civil Rights Movement," *Washington Post*, March 31, 2021.

CIVIL RIGHTS, TRUMAN, AND ENTER TAIL GUNNER JOE

17 "The FBI had spied on every prominent black": Weiner, *Enemies*, 197.

17 "The NAACP leadership was always on the lookout": Transcript of "Blinding of Isaac Woodard."

18 "I spent three and a half years in service to my country": Isaac Woodard, speech, at Oak Hill Avenue AME Church, October 1946, Youngstown, OH, quoted in Richard Gergel, *Unexampled Courage: The Blinding of Sgt. Isaac Woodard and the*

Awakening of President Harry S. Truman ad Judge Waties Waring (New York: Farrar, Straus & Giroux, 2019).

18 "The matter of discrimination": A. Philip Randolph to Harry S. Truman, December 28, 1947, Desegregation of the Armed Forces Collection, Harry S. Truman Library. Randolph was a labor leader who founded the Brotherhood of the Sleeping Car Porters. During World War II, he persuaded Roosevelt to order fair hiring practices in war industries.

18 "If we must die for our country": Walter Naegle, interview with authors, July 14, 2020.

19 "When a Mayor and City Marshal": Harry S. Truman to Ernie Roberts, August 18, 1948, Harry S. Truman Library, quoted in DeNeen L. Brown, "How Harry S. Truman Went from Being a Racist to Desegrating the Military," *Washington Post*, July 26, 2018.

20 "My forebears were confederates": Margaret Truman, *Harry S. Truman* (New York: William Morrow, 1973), 392, quoted in McCullough, *Truman*, 588.

20 "Had Enough! To Err is Truman": Alonzo L. Hamby, "Harry S. Truman: Domestic Affairs," Miller Center, University of Virginia, millercenter.org/president /truman/domestic-affairs.

20 "What makes you think": *Washington Post*, December 4, 1946, and *New York Times*, December 6, 1946, quoted in Oshinsky, *Conspiracy So Immense*, 59.

21 "He is a muscular six-footer": Jack Alexander, "The Senate's Remarkable Upstart," *Saturday Evening Post*, August 9, 1947.

TEACHERS, BEWARE

22 "Teachers saw children coming to school hungry": Clarence Taylor, interview with authors, January 23, 2019.

23 "The teaching profession as a whole": Frances Eisenberg in *Red Scare: Memories of the American Inquisition; An Oral History*, ed. Griffin Fariello (New York: Norton, 1995), 462.

23 "Become plumbers, become anything": Eisenberg in *Red Scare*, 462.

23 "It was a shame that teachers": Taylor interview, January 23, 2019.

23 "My six years as a teacher": Alex Kingsbury, "How the Red Scare Destroyed a Small-Town Teacher," *Boston Globe*, February 4, 2016.

23 "The mind of a child is particularly receptive": Kingsbury, "How Red Scare Destroyed Teacher."

24 "Rumor and gossip have had a field day": Kingsbury, "How Red Scare Destroyed Teacher."

ARE COMMUNISTS HIDING IN HOLLYWOOD?

26 "[HUAC was] interested in finding out": Clyde Tolson to J. Edgar Hoover, FBI memo 61–7582–1462, May 12, 1947, quoted in Theoharis, *From the Secret Files*, 112.

27 "Despite . . . being Washington's largest hearing room": "Red Probe on Today; 50 Called," *Hollywood Reporter*, October 20, 1947, quoted in Brimner, *Blacklisted!*, 20.

27 "The thing that I resent the most": The exchange between Disney and Smith is from *Hearings Regarding the Communist Infiltration of the Motion Picture Industry: Hearings Before the Committee on Un-American Activities, House of Representatives*, 80th Cong. 285 (October 24, 1947) (testimony of Walter E. Disney).

28 "Mr. Chairman, I have a statement": The following exchange of Lawson, Thomas, and Stripling is from *Communist Infiltration of Motion-Picture Industry Hearings*, 290, 292–95 (October 27, 1947) (testimony of John Howard Lawson).

29 "For a week, this Committee has conducted": John Howard Lawson, unread statement to House Un-American Activities Committee, quoted in Gordon Kahn, *Hollywood on Trial: The Story of the 10 Who Were Indicted* (New York: Boni & Gaer, 1948), 72.

30 "Congress shall make no law": U.S. Const. amend. I.

31 "I shall ask various questions": The exchange between Stripling and Trumbo is from *Communist Infiltration of Motion-Picture Industry Hearings*, 330 (October 28, 1947) (testimony of Dalton Trumbo).

32 "It's a very simple question": The exchange between Thomas and Lardner is from *Communist Infiltration of Motion-Picture Industry Hearings*, 482 (October 30, 1947) (testimony of Ring Lardner Jr.).

33 "As far as I was concerned": Dalton Trumbo in *Hollywood on Trial*, documentary film directed by David Helpern, Cinema Associates/October Films, 1976.

RED LIST, GRAY LIST, EVERYBODY'S GOT A LIST

34 "AMERICANS: DON'T PATRONIZE REDS!": Cinema Educational Guild pamphlet, ca. 1957, quoted in Karl Cohen, "Toontown's Reds: HUAC's Investigation of

Alleged Communists in the Animation Industry," *Film History* 5, no. 2 (June 1993): 193, jstor.org/stable/27670720.

34 "People are very much wrought up": Harry S. Truman to George Earle, February 28, 1947, quoted in Associated Press, "Earle Says Astonished at Truman," *Indiana* (PA) *Gazette*, April 3, 1947.

35 "The Republicans have tried": Clark M. Clifford to Harry S. Truman, memo, p. 15, November 19, 1947, 1948 Election Campaign Collection, Harry S. Truman Library, trumanlibrary.gov/library/research-files/memo-clark-clifford-harry-s-truman.

35 "I believe I speak": Harry S. Truman, statement on the government's Employee Loyalty Program, November 14, 1947, in *Public Papers of the Presidents of the United States: Harry S. Truman, 1947* (Washington, D.C.: Government Printing Office, 1963), 489.

36 "Here is a round dozen": "Big List of Red Fronts," *Times-Herald* (Washington D.C.), December 8, 1947, quoted in Robert Justin Goldstein, "Prelude to McCarthyism: The Making of a Blacklist," *Prologue*, Fall 2006, archives.gov/publications /prologue/2006/fall/agloso.html.

36 "Once the precedent is set": J. Edgar Hoover to Attorney General Tom C. Clark, memo, January 27, 1948, quoted in Morgan, *Reds*, 312.

36 "My father was a paid organizer": Josh interview, July 18, 2018.

37 "Neighbors informed on neighbors": Fariello, preface to *Red Scare*, 25.

38 "When Robin Hood (who I had always loved)": "Green Feather Movement," November 18, 2013, Teaching for Change, teachingforchange.org/green-feather -movement.

38 "Anything that disrupts law and order": United Press, "Indiana Censor Fears Little Red Robin Hood," *New York Times*, November 14, 1953.

38 "The best antidote to communism": *Investigation of Un-American Propaganda Activities in the United States: Hearings Before the Committee on Un-American Activities, House of Representatives*, part 2, 80th Cong., 43 (March 26, 1947) (testimony of J. Edgar Hoover, FBI director).

39 "Whenever any form of government": Declaration of Independence, National Archives, archives.gov/founding-docs/declaration-transcript.

40 "Communists . . . can teach our youth": Hoover testimony in *Un-American Propaganda Hearings*, 43.

40 "Freedom of speech may be taken away": George Washington, "To Officers of the Army," Newburgh, NY, March 15, 1783, Founders Online, National Archives, founders.archives.gov/documents/Washington/99–01–02–10840.

REAL PEOPLE, REAL FEAR

41 "There are few Americans": Francis J. McNamara, "What the Attorney General's List Means," *Elks Magazine*, November 1956, 14, quoted in Goldstein, "Prelude to McCarthyism."

41 "There is suspicion in the record": Loyalty questions are pulled from L. A. Nikolorić, "The Government Loyalty Program," *American Scholar* 19, no. 3 (Summer 1950): 294, jstor.org/stable/41205316.

42 "My parents left their jobs in television": Peter Frank, interview with authors, September 28, 2019.

42 "We were lucky": Joe Gilford, interview with authors, April 5, 2019.

43 "When I first discovered the blacklist": Harry Belafonte in *Scandalize My Name: Stories from the Black List*, documentary written and directed by Alexandra M. Isles, 3DD Entertainment, 1998.

44 "I said to him that many of the things": Belafonte in *Scandalize My Name* documentary.

44 "My parents were proud": Gilford interview.

44 "We figured we would go crazy": Ossie Davis in *Scandalize My Name* documentary.

44 "White Americans praised him": Martin Duberman, introduction to *Paul Robeson: No One Can Silence Me; Adapted for Young Adults* (New York: New Press, 2021).

45 "My father was on honor guard": Toby Emmer, interview with authors, April 1, 2019.

46 "By the time we came out of prison in 1951": Ring Lardner Jr. in *Red Scare*, 264.

47 "[Robin Hood is] a man who'll be remembered": "The Ordeal," *The Adventures of Robin Hood*, Series 1, Episode 11, screenplay by Ring Lardner Jr. (writing as Eric Heath), 1955, dailymotion.com/video/x3djk5r.

THE BERLIN AIRLIFT AND THE START OF POLITICS ON TV

48 "Television adds to the interest": Jack Gould, "Television and Politics," *New York Times*, July 18, 1948.

49 "I'll never forget my first flight": Suzanne Perez Tobias, "'Candy Bomber,' Now 94, Meets German Teen Who Found His Chocolate After WWII," *Wichita Eagle*, May 14, 2015, kansas.com/news/local/article21040404.html.

49 "You kept us alive": Steve Liewer, "'You Kept Us Alive': Berlin Airlift Veterans Meet in Omaha on 70th Anniversary," *Omaha World-Herald*, September 29, 2018.

49 "Only a miracle": Ernest K. Lindley, "The Republican Ticket and the Democrats," *Newsweek*, July 5, 1948, 20.

49 "Frankly, he's a gone goose": Clare Boothe Luce, speech before the Republican National Convention, Philadelphia, June 21, 1948, quoted in Doris Greenberg, "Mrs. Luce Attacks Truman and Party," *New York Times*, June 22, 1948.

50 "You could cut the gloom": Alben W. Barkley, *That Reminds Me*—(Garden City, NY: Doubleday, 1954), 200. [Barkley would be Truman's running mate and vice president from 1949 to 1953.]

50 "I was 17 years old": The exchange between Hal Rosenthal and the woman in the bar is adapted from Amy V. Simmons, "The First Televised Democratic Convention, 70 Years Later: An Unplanned Delegate Remembers," *Philadelphia Sunday Sun*, August 5, 2016, philasun.com/local/first-televised-democratic-convention-70-years-later-unplanned-delegate-remembers/.

51 "So there I was": Simmons, "First Televised Democratic Convention."

51 "To those who say we are rushing": Hubert Humphrey, speech on civil rights, Democratic National Convention, Philadelphia, July 14, 1948, audio recording, Hubert H. Humphrey Papers, Minnesota Historical Society, mnhs.org/library/findaids/01098/audio/01098_00102.mp3.

52 "You shall not crucify the South": Charles J. Bloch, speech nominating Richard B. Russell to be president of the United States, Democratic National Convention, Philadelphia, July 14, 1948, reprinted in 94 Cong. Rec. (July 28, 1948), app. pt. 12, A4713.

53 "Harry Truman's a goddamn liar": D. B. Hardeman and Donald C. Bacon, *Rayburn: A Biography* (Austin: Texas Monthly Press, 1987), 338.

COMMUNIST SPIES AND TRUMAN LOSES (OR DOES HE?)

54 "We have been stabbed in the back": John N. Popham, "Southerners Name Thurmond to Lead Anti-Truman Fight," *New York Times*, July 18, 1948.

54 "There is political dynamite": David McCullough, *Truman* (New York: Simon & Schuster, 1992), 652.

55 "For a number of years I had myself served": *Hearings Regarding Communist Espionage in the United States Government: Hearings Before the Committee on Un-American Activities, House of Representatives*, 80th Cong., 565 (August 3, 1948) (testimony of Whittaker Chambers, senior editor at *Time* magazine).

55 "I am here at my own request": *Communist Espionage Hearings*, 642 (August 5, 1948) (testimony of Alger Hiss).

55 "Mr. President, do you think": Question and answer from news conference, August 5, 1948, in *Public Papers of the Presidents: Harry S. Truman, 1948* (Washington, D.C.: Government Printing Office, 1964), 432–33.

56 "The FBI helped Dewey": William C. Sullivan, *The Bureau: My 30 Years in Hoover's FBI*, with Bill Brown (New York: Norton, 1979), 44, quoted in McCullough, *Truman*, 673.

56 "Communists and fellow travelers": "Dogi Cligin and the West," National Affairs, *Time*, October 4, 1948, quoted in McCullough, *Truman*, 674.

56 "The landslide for Dewey": "Election Forecast: 50 Political Experts Predict a GOP Sweep," *Newsweek*, October 11, 1948, 20.

57 "Mr. Truman is the most complete fumbler": "And Now, the Ballot Box!," editorial, *Los Angeles Times*, October 31, 1948.

58 "He is good on the back of a train": Sam Rayburn to Robert L. Holliday, June 19, 1948, quoted in Hardeman and Bacon, *Rayburn*, 339–40.

THE PERFECT MAN TO LIGHT THE FIRE

60 "President Truman was blamed": Sam Rushay, "Harry Truman and Revolution in China, 1949," *Examiner* (Independence, MO), June 7, 2014.

61 "We deplore the dangerous degree": 96 Cong. Rec. 1542 (February 7, 1950).

62 "I have here in my hand a list": Joe McCarthy, prepared script of Lincoln Day address, Wheeling, WV, February 9, 1950, in *State Department Employee Loyalty Investigation: Hearings Before a Subcommittee of the Committee on Foreign Relations, U.S. Senate*, 81st Cong., app., 1765 (1950) (affidavit of James K. Whitaker, news editor of WWVA).

62 *Wheeling Intelligencer* anecdote: Halberstam, *Fifties*, 50.

63 "He grasped something": Tye, *Demagogue*, 115.

63 "Left Commie list in other bag": "57 Reds Help Shaping U.S. Policy: McCarthy," *Denver Post*, February 11, 1950.

63 "He lost his list between": Bayley, *McCarthy and the Press*, 30.

63 "I just want you to know": Bayley, *McCarthy and the Press*, 36.

64 "Your board did a painstaking job": Senator Joseph R. McCarthy to President Harry S. Truman, telegram, February 11, 1950, President's Secretary's Files (Truman Administration), 1945–1960, National Archives, catalog.archives.gov/id/201514.

64 "I read your telegram": Truman to McCarthy, undated response to February 11 telegram [unsent], President's Secretary's Files (Truman Administration), 1945–1960, National Archives, catalog.archives.gov/id/201514.

65 "No one need ever erect": Joe McCarthy to Edgar Hoover, July 30, 1952, FBI FOIA Vault, quoted in Oshinsky, *Conspiracy So Immense*, 257.

65 "Don't ever use specific figures": Adapted from Curt Gentry, *J. Edgar Hoover: The Man and the Secrets* (New York: Norton, 1991), 378.

65 "Review the files" and "We didn't have enough evidence": Gentry, *J. Edgar Hoover*, 379.

66 "Will the Senator from Wisconsin": The exchange between Lehman and McCarthy is from 96 Cong. Rec. 4380 (March 30, 1950).

66 "Go back to your seat, old man" and "Lehman looked all around": Stewart Alsop, *The Center: People and Power in Political Washington* (New York: Harper & Row, 1968), 8–9.

68 "Margaret, you look very serious": The exchange between McCarthy and Margaret Chase Smith is from Oshinsky, *Conspiracy So Immense*, 164.

69 "I would like to speak briefly": 96 Cong. Rec. 7894–95 (June 1, 1950) (speech of Senator Margaret Chase Smith of Maine).

70 Snow White: Oshinsky, *Conspiracy So Immense*, 215.

DUCK AND COVER: RUSSIA GETS THE BOMB

71 "We have evidence": Harry S. Truman, "Statement by the President Announcing the First Atomic Explosion in the USSR," September 23, 1949, in *Public Papers of*

the Presidents: Harry S. Truman, 1949 (Washington, D.C.: Government Printing Office, 1964), 485.

71 "Truman Says Russia Set Off Atom Blast": *Sun* (New York), September 24, 1949.

71 "Truman Reports Atomic Blast in Russia": *Evening Star* (Washington, D.C.), September 23, 1949.

71 "Part of America's obsession": David Munns, interview with the authors, March 19, 2019.

72 "We all know the atomic bomb": *Duck and Cover*, Federal Civil Defense Administration film, 1951, youtu.be/IKqXu-5jw60.

72 "Remember what to do, friends": *Duck and Cover* film.

74 "The Venona messages were encoded": Liza Mundy, "The Women Code Breakers Who Unmasked Soviet Spies," *Smithsonian Magazine*, September 2018, smithsonianmag.com/history/women-code-breakers-unmasked-soviet-spies-180970034/.

74 "According to transcripts": Katherine L. Herbig and Martin F. Wiskoff, *Espionage Against the United States by American Citizens 1947–2001* (Monterey, CA: Defense Personnel Security Research Center, 2002), 5, sgp.fas.org/library/spies.pdf.

74 "She gives the impression": John Earl Haynes, Harvey Klehr, and Alexander Vassiliev, *Spies: The Rise and Fall of the KGB in America* (New Haven, CT: Yale University Press, 2009), 288, quoted in Weiner, *Enemies*, 163. This memo was not a Venona cable but a document in the KGB archives transcribed by Vassiliev.

74 "The Venona documents themselves": Ellen Schrecker and Phillip Deery, *The Age of McCarthyism: A Brief History with Documents*, 3rd ed. (Boston: Bedford/St. Martin's, 2016), 128.

75 "It wasn't until seventeen years later": Emily Socolov, interview with authors, February 18, 2021.

75 "Nothing that happened": Robert J. Lamphere and Tom Shachtman, *The FBI-KGB War: A Special Agent's Story* (Macon, GA: Mercer University Press, 1995), 123.

POLICE ACTION IN KOREA

76 "Seventy percent of Americans think": George H. Gallup, *The Gallup Poll: Public Opinion, 1935–1971*, vol. 2, *1949–1958* (New York: Random House, 1972), 881, 916, 919.

77 "N. Korea Reds Declare War": *Daily News* (New York), June 25, 1950.

78 "If the best minds in the world": Joseph C. Goulden, *Korea, the Untold Story of the War* (New York: Times Books, 1982), 3, quoted in Halberstam, *The Fifties*, 62.

78 "I was a high school dropout": Adapted from Charles Rangel, interview by Jongwoo Han, May 28, 2013, Korean War Legacy Foundation, youtu.be /3WSqlFLHUI0.

79 "It was so cold": Arden Rowley speech, Korean War Legacy Foundation, korean warlegacy.org/interviews/arden-rowley/.

79 "What to do with Mr. Prima Donna": Harry S. Truman, longhand note, June 17, 1945, Harry S. Truman Papers: President's Secretary's Files, Harry S. Truman Library, trumanlibrary.gov/library/truman-papers/longhand-notes-presidential -file-1944–1953/june-17-and-july-4–1945.

79 "MacArthur is as big a baby": Dwight D. Eisenhower, January 19 and 23, 1942, January-July 1942 diary, Dwight D. Eisenhower Presidential Library, eisenhower library.gov/research/online-documents/diaries-dwight-d-eisenhower.

80 "When the Chinese hit": Rangel interview, Korean War Legacy Foundation.

80 "The communist forces": Arden Rowley speech, Korean War Legacy Foundation, koreanwarlegacy.org/interviews/arden-rowley/.

81 "I was ready to kick him": Margaret Truman, *Harry S. Truman* (New York: William Morrow, 1973), 513.

THE ROSENBERG SPY CASE

83 "Has this infiltration": Patrick McCarran, "Communist Threat Inside U.S.: Interview with Senator McCarran," *U.S. News and World Report*, November 16, 1951, 29.

83 "The McCarran Act reflected": Oshinsky, *Conspiracy So Immense*, 173.

83 "[Communists] are noisy": Harry S. Truman, "Address at a Dinner of the Federal Bar Association," April 24, 1950, *Public Papers of the Presidents*, 272.

84 "Ethel and Jules were just": Jean Le Bec, interview with authors, April 28, 2020.

84 "On July 17, 1950": Robert Meeropol and Michael Meeropol, *We Are Your Sons: The Legacy of Ethel and Julius Rosenberg* (Boston: Houghton Mifflin, 1975), 5.

85 "None of the 'secrets'": Munns interview, March 19, 2019.

85 "After the Rosenbergs were arrested": Le Bec interview, April 28, 2020.

86 "Roy looked scary to me": Dave Marcus, interview with authors, April 25, 2019.

86 "We didn't want them to die": Daniel F. Gilmore, United Press International, "Julius and Ethel Rosenberg, Revisited," *Sacramento Bee*, June 18, 1978.

86 "I remember my sister": Le Bec interview, April 28, 2020.

87 "We can elect": Joe McCarthy to Tom Korb, January 8, 1951, Korb Papers, quoted in Reeves, *Life of McCarthy*, 346.

87 "Anybody is a damn fool": C. L. Sulzberger, diary, May 12, 1952, in *A Long Row of Candles: Memoirs and Diaries, 1934–1954* (Toronto: Macmillan, 1969), 752, quoted in Halberstam, *Fifties*, 210.

88 "Joe never plans": Emmet John Hughes diary, July 16, 1953, Seeley G. Mudd Manuscript Library, Princeton University, quoted in David A. Nichols, *Ike and McCarthy: Dwight Eisenhower's Secret Campaign Against Joseph McCarthy* (New York: Simon & Schuster, 2017), 14.

88 "Humility must always be": Dwight D. Eisenhower, Guildhall Address, London, June 12, 1945, audio recording, Dwight D. Eisenhower Presidential Library, eisenhowerlibrary.gov/eisenhowers/speeches.

88 "My good friends": *Official Report of the Proceedings of the Twenty-Fifth Republican National Convention . . .* (Washington, D.C., [1952]), 142–47, quoted in Reeves, *Life of McCarthy*, 426.

89 "He is getting skilled advice": Miles McMillin, "Sen. McCarthy Shows Skill in TV Techniques," *Capital Times* (Madison, WI), July 10, 1952.

89 "A Republican President": Republican Party Platform of 1952 Online, eds. Gerhard Peters and John T. Woolley, American Presidency Project, presidency.ucsb.edu/node/273395.

90 "Do you favor the reelection": Question and Eisenhower's answer are from "The Transcript of General Eisenhower's First Press Conference Giving His Political Views," *New York Times*, June 6, 1952.

90 "Yes, I guess almost everybody": John B. Oakes, "Report on McCarthy and McCarthyism," *New York Times Magazine*, November 2, 1952, 12.

90 "Joe treats the Communist party": Oakes, "McCarthy and McCarthyism," 28.

90 "Pimple on path of progress": James C. Hagerty, diary, March 8, 1954, McCarthyism/"Red Scare" online documents, Dwight D. Eisenhower Presidential Library, eisenhowerlibrary.gov/research/online-documents/mccarthyism-red-scare.

91 "The whole notion of loyalty inquisitions": Adlai Stevenson, veto message, June 26, 1951, *The Papers of Adlai E. Stevenson*, ed. Walter Johnson, vol. 3, *Governor of*

Illinois, 1949–1953 (Boston: Little, Brown, 1973), 416, 418, quoted in Oshinsky, *Conspiracy So Immense*, 227.

91 "What the hell are you doing?": Question and McCarthy's answer are from Samuel Shaffer, *On and Off the Floor: Thirty Years as a Correspondent on Capitol Hill* (New York: Newsweek Books, 1980), 43, quoted in Oshinsky, *Conspiracy So Immense*, 232.

92 "I Like Ike" animated television commercial for Republican presidential candidate Dwight D. Eisenhower, produced by Roy Disney and Citizens for Eisenhower during the 1952 U.S. presidential campaign. Archival footage supplied by the Internet Moving Images Archive (at archive.org) in association with Prelinger Archives.

AN EXECUTION

93 "Let us have no part": Dorothy Day, "Meditation on the Death of the Rosenbergs," *Catholic Worker*, July-August 1953, 6.

94 "The execution of two human beings": Dwight D. Eisenhower, "Statement Declining to Intervene on Behalf of Julius and Ethel Rosenberg," June 19, 1953, in *Public Papers of the Presidents: Dwight D. Eisenhower, 1953* (Washington, D.C.: U.S. Government Printing Office, 1960), 447.

95 "Just because Julius Rosenberg": Alan M. Dershowitz, "Rosenbergs Were Guilty—and Framed," commentary, *Los Angeles Times*, July 19, 1995.

95 "Great": Dershowitz, "Rosenbergs Were Guilty."

95 "Dearest sweethearts": Meeropol and Meeropol, *We Are Your Sons*, 235.

96 "Their lips defiantly sealed": Jack Woliston, "The Rosenbergs Go Silently to the Electric Chair," United Press International Archives, June 20, 1953, upi.com /Archives/1953/06/20/Rosenbergs-go-silently-to-electric-chair/5084629411212/.

BATMAN GETS HIS ROBIN, AND ROBIN GETS HIS ROBIN

97 "Some people don't realize it": Harvey Matusow, *False Witness* (New York: Cameron & Kahn, 1955), 146, quoted in Reeves, *Life of McCarthy*, 434.

98 "Roy is one of the most brilliant": Reeves, *Life of McCarthy*, 465.

98 "he was going so fast": Ruth Young Watt, interview by Donald A. Ritchie, September 21, 1979, transcript, 111, Women of the Senate Oral History Project,

Senate Historical Office, senate.gov/artandhistory/history/oral_history/Ruth _Young_Watt.htm.

98 "Wealth, of course, is not out of place": "Schine at Harvard: Boy with the Baton," *Harvard Crimson*, May 7, 1954.

99 "Dave Schine turned out to be": "The Self-Inflated Target," National Affairs, *Time*, March 22, 1954, 26.

99 "Dave was never on the payroll": Watt oral history, 107.

99 "In order to avoid": U.S. International Information Administration, "Background Information Relating to the IIA Instruction of the Use of Materials by Controversial Persons," summary memorandum in *Foreign Relations of the United States, 1952–1954, National Security Affairs*, vol. 2, pt. 2, eds. Lisle A. Rose, Neal H. Petersen, and William Z. Slany (Washington, DC: Government Printing Office, 1984), 1678, history.state.gov/historicaldocuments/frus1952–54v02p2/d319.

100 "The staff was very apprehensive": Francis O. Wilcox, interview by Donald A. Ritchie, March 21, 1984, transcript, 109, Oral History Project, Senate Historical Office, senate.gov/artandhistory/history/oral_history/Francis_O_Wilcox.htm.

100 "Scummy snoopers": Drew Pearson, "Odd Antics of McCarthy's Investigators in Europe," Washington Merry-Go-Round, *St. Louis Post-Dispatch*, April 22, 1953.

100 "Their limited vocabulary": "'Something Wrong' If Welcome Is Cool," *Manchester Guardian* (UK), April 20, 1953.

100 "The two junior G-men": Pearson, Washington Merry-Go-Round, April 22, 1953.

101 "Once the dogs are set": Associated Press, "Text of Letter Left by 'Voice' Suicide," *New York Times*, March 7, 1953, quoted in Oshinsky, *Conspiracy So Immense*, 271.

102 "The State Department's book-burning": Joseph and Stewart Alsop, "The Book Burners," Matter of Fact, *Wilkes-Barre Record* (PA), June 17, 1953.

102 "was a colossal mistake": Cohn, *McCarthy*, 81.

102 "Senator McCarthy is": Dwight D. Eisenhower, April 1, 1953, August 1952– August 1953 diary, Dwight D. Eisenhower Presidential Library, eisenhowerlibrary .gov/research/online-documents/diaries-dwight-d-eisenhower.

103 "Don't join the book burners": Dwight D. Eisenhower, remarks at the Dartmouth College commencement, June 14, 1953, in *Public Papers of the Presidents*, 411.

104 "He's the sorriest senator": Bobby Baker, *Wheeling and Dealing: Confessions of a Capitol Hill Operator*, with Larry L. King (New York: W. W. Norton, 1978), 94.

104 "McCarthy was such an evil": Milton S. Eisenhower, oral history interview by John Luter, September 6, 1967, transcript, 65, Eisenhower Administration Project, Columbia Center for Oral History, Columbia University, dlc.library.columbia .edu/time_based_media/10.7916/d8-yf1t-2120.

105 "You want me" and "loathed McCarthy": William Bragg Ewald Jr., *Who Killed Joe McCarthy?* (New York: Simon & Schuster, 1984), 66, 67.

105 "Our librarians serve": Dwight D. Eisenhower, "Letter on Intellectual Freedom to the President of the American Library Association," June 26, 1953, in *Public Papers of the Presidents*, 455.

106 "WHEREAS the interests": Executive Order 10450, "Security Requirements for Government Employment," 18 Fed. Reg. 2489, no. 82 (April 29, 1953), archives .gov/federal-register/codification/executive-order/10450.html.

106 "J. Edgar Hoover says": Christopher M. Elias, *Gossip Men: J. Edgar Hoover, Joe McCarthy, Roy Cohn, and the Politics of Insinuation* (The University of Chicago Press, 2021), 148.

107 "Who could be more dangerous": 96 Cong. Rec. 5699 (April 25, 1950) (exchange between Senator Kenneth Wherry of Nebraska and Senator William Jenner of Indiana).

107 "All too often we lose sight": Eugene D. Williams, introduction to *The Sexual Criminal: A Psychoanalytical Study*, by J. Paul de River (Springfield, IL: Charles C. Thomas, 1949).

107 "I shall continue": 96 Cong. Rec. 5712 (April 25, 1950) (remarks of Senator Wherry).

108 "You will find that practically": 96 Cong. Rec. 1961 (February 20, 1950).

109 "They swooped in": Josh Howard, dir., *The Lavender Scare*, documentary film, 77 mins., Full Exposure Films, 2017.

109 "Bayard was comfortable": Walter Naegle, interview with authors, July 14, 2020.

109 "Dr. King came from": Bayard Rustin, "Time on Two Crosses: An Interview with Goerge Chauncey Jr." in *Time on Two Crosses: Collected Writings of Bayard Rustin*, eds. Devon W. Carbado and Donald Weise (San Francisco: Cleis Press, 2004), 302.

109 "Dr. King was never": Bayard Rustin, "Black and Gay in the Civil Rights Movement: An Interview with Open Hands" in *Time on Two Crosses*, 285.

110 "Scientists and their friends": Edward Shils, "Security and Science Sacrificed to Loyalty," *Bulletin of the Atomic Scientists* 11, no 4 (April 1955): 106, 108.

110 "It was no accident": David K. Johnson, *Lavender Scare*, 181.

110 "We have information": The exchange with bureaucrats is from Frank Kameny, interview with Eric Marcus, June 3, 1989, audio recording, *Making Gay History: The Podcast*, makinggayhistory.com/podcast/episode-1–5/.

111 "Why has Washington gone crazy?": Joseph and Stewart Alsop, "Why Has Washington Gone Crazy?," *Saturday Evening Post*, July 29, 1950.

111 "I know some": 96 Cong. Rec. 11979 (August 8, 1950) (removal of sexual perverts from government employment).

112 "My father and uncle": Elizabeth Winthrop, interview with authors, August 8, 2020.

I LOVE LUCY AND *SEE IT NOW*

113 "Tonight we greet": Dwight D. Eisenhower, "Radio and Television Address to the American People Announcing the Signing of the Korean Armistice," July 26, 1953, in *Public Papers of the Presidents*, 520.

114 "We had a very bad feeling": *Investigation of Communist Activities in the Los Angeles Area—Part 7: Hearing Before the Committee on Un-American Activities, House of Representatives*, 83rd Cong., 1567 (September 4, 1953) (testimony of Lucille Désirée Ball Arnaz).

115 "The nation's reservoirs": Darin Strauss, "The 'Wildcat' Episode, or, Did Broadway Love Lucy?," *New York Times*, July 31, 2020.

115 "While *I Love Lucy* is being shown": Bart Andrews, *Lucy & Ricky & Fred & Ethel: The Story of "I Love Lucy"* (New York: E. P. Dutton, 1976), 2–3.

115 "I can still recall": Fred Friendly, foreword to *To Strike at a King: The Turning Point in the McCarthy Witch-Hunts*, by Michael Ranville (Troy, MI: Momentum Books, 1997).

116 "Good evening": The following quotes by Murrow, Fishman, Radulovich, and Wershba are from the transcript of "The Case of Lieutenant Milo Radulovich," episode aired October 20, 1953, in Edward R. Murrow and Fred Friendly, eds., *See It Now* (New York: Simon & Schuster, 1955), 30, 36.

119 "What would you say if I told you": Joseph Wershba, "Murrow vs. McCarthy: See It Now," *New York Times Magazine*, March 4, 1979, 33, quoted in Oshinsky, *Conspiracy So Immense*, 398.

SPIES IN NEW JERSEY

120 "Rosenberg Called Radar Spy Leader": Edward Ranzal, "Rosenberg Called Radar Spy Leader," *New York Times*, October 16, 1953.

122 "Hoover wrote me": Robin Bady, interview with authors, March 18, 2020.

122 "It has all the earmarks": "Spying Is Charged at Fort Monmouth," *New York Times*, October 13, 1953; Associated Press, "Army Secretary Attends Radar Espionage Probe," *Minneapolis Star*, October 13, 1953.

122 "There were no screams": Bady interview, March 20, 2020.

123 "No information shall be supplied": The exchange between McCarthy and General Reber is pulled from *Army Civilian Workers Hearings* (testimony of Major General Miles Reber), 9, 12, 15, and 16, quoted in Oshinsky, *Conspiracy So Immense*, 332–33.

124 "This is war!": John G. Adams, *Without Precedent: The Story of the Death of McCarthyism* (New York: W. W. Norton, 1983), 76, quoted in Nichols, *Ike and McCarthy*, 77.

124 "give a tinker's dam": United Press, "McCarthy Attacks 'Bleeding Hearts,'" *New York Times*, October 28, 1953.

125 "Even though my father got his job back": Bady interview, March 20, 2020.

COHN GOES TOO FAR, AND THE WHITE HOUSE SETS A TRAP

126 "David Schine had been classified 4-F": Tom Wolfe, "Dangerous Obsessions," review of *The Autobiography of Roy Cohn* by Sidney Zion (Secaucus, NJ: Lyle Stuart, 1988) and *Citizen Cohn* by Nicholas von Hoffman (New York: Doubleday, 1988), *New York Times Book Review*, April 3, 1988, 24.

126 "I received numerous telephone calls": *Special Senate Investigation on Charges and Countercharges Involving: Secretary of the Army Robert T. Stevens, John G. Adams, H. Struve Hensel and Senator Joe McCarthy, Roy M. Cohn, and Francis P. Carr: Hearings Before the United States Senate Committee on Government Operations, Special Subcommittee on Investigations* [hereafter *Army-McCarthy Hearings*], 83rd Cong., 40, 52 (April 22, 1954) (testimony of Major General Miles Reber).

127 "Cohn made calls to everyone": Wolfe, "Dangerous Obsessions," April 3, 1988.

127 "The Army is making Dave": Adams, *Without Precedent*, 83, quoted in Nichols, *Ike and McCarthy*, 101.

127 "I would like to ask you": Record of monitored phone call November 7, 1953, read in *Army-McCarthy Hearings*, 2150–51 (June 7, 1954), quoted in Rovere, *Senator Joe McCarthy*, 207.

128 "I'll teach you": Adams, *Without Precedent*, 84.

129 "Senator McCarthy has attacked": Stanley M. Rumbough Jr. and Charles Masterson to Murray Snyder (assistant White House press secretary), memorandum, December 1, 1953, McCarthyism/"Red Scare" online documents, Dwight D. Eisenhower Presidential Library, eisenhowerlibrary.gov/research/online-documents/mccarthyism-red-scare.

McCARTHY HUNTS FOR COMMIES AND BAGS A DENTIST

131 "The dread secret": Dwight D. Eisenhower, "Address Before the General Assembly of the United Nations on Peaceful Uses of Atomic Energy," New York City, December 8, 1953, in *Public Papers of the Presidents*, 816–17, 820.

131 "President Eisenhower's overture": William S. White, "President's Talk Weakens Critics," *New York Times*, December 10, 1953.

131 "It is both typical" and "a captain or a major": Adams, *Without Precedent*, 116, quoted in Nichols, *Ike and McCarthy*, 88.

132 "Did anyone in the Army": The exchange between McCarthy and Peress is from *Communist Infiltration in the Army: Hearings Before the United States Senate Committee on Government Operations, Permanent Subcommittee on Investigations*, 83rd Cong., 110–11 (January 30, 1954) (testimony of Major Irving Peress).

133 "Senator Joe McCarthy, after a fortnight": "The Oak and the Ivy," Investigations, *Time*, March 8, 1954, 21.

133 "Did you know that he refused": The exchange between McCarthy and Zwicker is pulled from *Communist Infiltration in the Army Hearings*, 147–48, 151, 153–54 (February 18, 1954) (testimony of Brigadier General Ralph W. Zwicker).

136 "Have you a record of this?": The exchange between Sherman Adams and John Adams is from John Adams, *Without Precedent*, 112–13.

136 "atomic weapon": Nicholas von Hoffman, *Citizen Cohn* (New York: Doubleday, 1988), 218.

137 "The luncheon meeting": Oshinsky, *Conspiracy So Immense*, 385.

137 "Stevens couldn't have conceded": "McCarthy's 'Bumbling Target,'" sidebar in "The Men at the Top: The Story of J. P. Stevens," *Southern Exposure: Packaging the New South*, v6 n1, 60.

138 "By supinely capitulating": "McCarthy Rides Again," editorial, *Richmond* (VA) *News Leader*, February 25, 1954.

138 "It seems to us": "McCarthy and Zwicker," editorial, *Chicago Tribune*, February 25, 1954.

138 "Secretary of the Army Stevens denies": "The American Army Surrenders," editorial, February 25, 1954, *Milwaukee Journal*.

138 "Investigation of the Army": Henry Cabot Lodge to the president, February 23, 1954, Lodge-Eisenhower correspondence, Reel 28, Henry Cabot Lodge Papers, Massachusetts Historical Society, quoted in Allan J. Lichtman, *White Protestant Nation: The Rise of the American Conservative Movement* (New York: Atlantic Monthly Press, 2008), 191.

139 "The president seems": *RN: The Memoirs of Richard Nixon* (New York: Grosset & Dunlap, 1978), 149.

140 "Let's go out and grin": Legislative meeting, March 1, 1954, Dwight D. Eisenhower diary, B4, Staff Notes, Dwight D. Eisenhower Presidential Library, quoted in Nichols, *Ike and McCarthy*, 116.

140 "I talked to Pres. in gym": James C. Hagerty, diary, March 8, 1954, McCarthyism/ "Red Scare" online documents, Dwight D. Eisenhower Presidential Library, eisen howerlibrary.gov/research/online-documents/mccarthyism-red-scare.

140 "That the weapon": Von Hoffman, *Citizen Cohn*, 218.

140 "It would be quicker" and "He agreed": Adams, *Without Precedent*, 122–23.

141 "In opposing communism": Dwight D. Eisenhower, press conference, March 3, 1954, *Public Papers of the Presidents: Dwight D. Eisenhower, 1954* (Washington, D.C.: U.S. Government Printing Office, 1960), 289.

141 "Why, the yellow son of a bitch": William Edwards, "Press Conference Notes," n.d., quoted in Oshinsky, *Conspiracy So Immense*, 392.

141 "If a stupid, arrogant": Associated Press, "Texts of Statements by President and Senator McCarthy's Reply," *New York Times*, March 4, 1954.

141 "President Eisenhower turned": James Reston, "Other Cheek Is Struck," *New York Times*, March 4, 1954.

142 "Extremism produces extremism": "Adlai Asks: Is Ike's New Look Leaving Us Defenseless to Red Nibbling?" *The Boston Globe*, March 7, 1954.

142 "Stevenson Says President": John Popham, "Stevenson Says President Yields to McCarthyism," *New York Times*, March 7, 1954.

142 "I think we probably": *Memoirs of Richard Nixon*, 144, quoted in Nichols, *Ike and McCarthy*, 181.

143 "When you go out and shoot rats": *Memoirs of Richard Nixon*, 146.

143 "That prick Nixon": Urban Van Susteren, interview, November 25, 1975, Wisconsin State Historical Society, pp. 3–4, quoted in Herman, *McCarthy: Most Hated Senator*, 300.

143 "The word 'invisible'": Oshinsky, *Conspiracy So Immense*, 395.

144 "This brief talk": 100 Cong. Rec. 2886 (March 9, 1954) (speech of Senator Ralph Flanders of Vermont).

144 "I think America needs": Dwight Eisenhower to Ralph Flanders, March 9, 1954, Office File, Eisenhower Library, quoted in Oshinsky, *Conspiracy So Immense*, 397.

JOE McCARTHY AND HIS TERRIBLE, HORRIBLE, NO GOOD, VERY BAD WEEK

145 "Tonight at 10:30": Advertisement, p. 34, *New York Times*, March 9, 1954.

145 "You know, the man" and "Will he take": Jimmy Breslin, "Ed Murrow's Plan: Let Joe McCarthy Destroy Self," *Boston Globe*, April 29, 1965.

146 "Ed could say 'twenty-six'": Joseph E. Persico, *Edward R. Murrow: An American Original* (New York: McGraw-Hill, 1988), 14.

146 "Good evening": "A Report on Senator Joseph R. McCarthy," produced and edited by Fred Friendly and Edward R. Murrow, *See It Now*, March 9, 1954, CBS-TV, transcript in supplementary readings for "The Beat Begins: America in the 1950s," seminar by Peter Losin and Michael Hall, plosin.com/beatbegins/archive/Murrow540309.htm.

147 "There was the high-pitched giggle": Persico, *Edward R. Murrow*, 378.

147 "Murrow plays a sound tape": Neil McDonald, "Trial by Television: The Downfall of Joseph MCarthy," *Quadrant* 50, no. 3 (March 2014): 90.

147 "We must remember": *See It Now* transcript, March 9, 1954.

147 "Send me your Commies": Alexander Kendrick, *Prime Time: The Life of Edward R. Murrow* (Boston: Little, Brown, 1969), 421, quoted in Reeves, *Life of McCarthy*, 565.

148 "Army report": James C. Hagerty, diary, March 11, 1954, Hagerty Papers, Dwight D. Eisenhower Presidential Library, quoted in William Bragg Ewald Jr., *Eisenhower the President: Crucial Days, 1951–1960* (Englewood Cliffs, NJ: Prentice-Hall, 1981), 133.

148 "Cohn has to go" and "It's blackmail": Charles E. Potter, *Days of Shame* (New York: Coward-McCann, 1965), 30, quoted in Oshinsky, *Conspiracy So Immense*, 401.

148 "Master though he was": Michael Straight, *Trial by Television* (Boston: Beacon Press, 1954), 82.

149 "The Army charged": United Press, "M'Carthy-Army Feud Explodes: 'Pressure' Charged to Senator," *Albuquerque Tribune*, March 12, 1954.

149 "At last McCarthy had been caught": Jack Anderson, *Confessions of a Muckraker: The Inside Story of Life in Washington During the Truman, Eisenhower, Kennedy and Johnson Years* (New York: Random House, 1979), 265.

ROY COHN PUNCHES BACK

150 "I don't answer charges": Oshinsky, *Conspiracy So Immense*, 405.

150 "Senator Joseph McCarthy declared tonight": W. H. Lawrence, "McCarthy Defends His Methods and Defies Critics High and Low," *New York Times*, March 18, 1954.

151 "Instead of our pressuring": Sidney Zion, *The Autobiography of Roy Cohn* (Secaucus, NJ: Lyle Stuart, 1988), 123.

151 "Senator Joseph R. McCarthy today angrily": W. H. Lawrence, "M'Carthy Charges Army 'Blackmail,'" *New York Times*, March 13, 1954.

151 "No improper influence": United Press, "'Blackmail' Is McCarthy Reply to Army," *Albuquerque Tribune*, March 12, 1954, quoted in Nichols, *Ike and McCarthy*, 201.

151 "I didn't say I would": Lawrence, "M'Carthy Charges Army 'Blackmail.'"

151 "Utterly untrue": Comments by both Secretary Stevens and John Adams are from Lawrence, "M'Carthy Charges Army 'Blackmail.'"

152 "President getting pretty sick": James C. Hagerty, diary, May 12, 1954, McCarthyism/"Red Scare" online documents, Eisenhower Library, eisenhowerlibrary.gov /research/online-documents/mccarthyism-red-scare.

152 "Someone is lying": *Washington Post*, March 13, 1954, quoted in Oshinsky, *Conspiracy So Immense*, 406.

152 "It is our baby": *Army-McCarthy Hearings*, 16 (March 16, 1954), quoted in Oshinsky, *Conspiracy So Immense*, 406.

152 "This is a little like": "The Senate Inquiry," editorial, *New York Times*, March 17, 1954.

152 "Ike wants hearings": James C. Hagerty, diary, May 11–12, 1954, Hagerty Papers, Eisenhower Library, quoted in Nichols, *Ike and McCarthy*, 207.

152 "I've made up my mind": Hagerty diary, March 24, 1954, McCarthyism/"Red Scare" online documents, Eisenhower Library.

THE ARMY-McCARTHY HEARINGS: TELEVISION SENSATION OF THE CENTURY

155 "At seven that morning": Straight, *Trial by Television*, 4–5.

156 "The reporters . . . kept asking": Oshinsky, *Conspiracy So Immense*, 409–10.

156 "Boys" and "Mr. Welch": *Army-McCarthy Hearings*, 2428 (June 9, 1954).

156 "count on a friend": Fred Fisher, unpublished manuscript, quoted in Nichols, *Ike and McCarthy*, 220, and Oshinsky, *Conspiracy So Immense*, 458.

157 "association was a different story": Hagerty diary, April 2, 1954, Hagerty Papers, Eisenhower Library, quoted in Ewald, *Eisenhower the President*, 135.

157 "Our counsel" and "A point of order": *Army-McCarthy Hearings*, 31 (April 22, 1954).

157 "McCarthy, ill-tempered": Straight, *Trial by Television*, 80.

158 "Television enabled": Haynes Johnson, *The Age of Anxiety: McCarthyism to Terrorism* (Orlando, FL: Harcourt, 2005), 389.

158 "Each afternoon": Straight, *Trial by Television*, 80.

158 "There was something": Joseph N. Welch, "The Lawyer's Afterthoughts," *Life*, July 26, 1954, 100.

159 "It is safe to assume": "After the Brawl," editorial, *Collier's*, August 6, 1954, 90.

159 "We've got the bastard": Robert Stevens, conversation with Ann Lousin, reported in email to David Nichols, May 25, 2013, quoted in Nichols, *Ike and McCarthy*, 287.

HAVE YOU NO SENSE OF DECENCY?

160 "He seemed rather like a cherub": Straight, *Trial by Television*, 80.

161 "There is something": The exchange between Cohn and Welch is from Cohn, *McCarthy*, 200, 202.

161 "We shook hands": Cohn, *McCarthy*, 202–3.

162 "May I add": Welch's words and those of McCarthy and Mundt are from *Army-McCarthy Hearings*, 2426–27 (June 9, 1954), content.wisconsinhistory.org/digital/collection/tp/id/55276.

162 "I think we should tell him": *Army-McCarthy Hearings*, 2427 (June 9, 1954).

162 "Roy Cohn grimaced": "Investigations," National Affairs, *Time*, June 21, 1954, 21.

162 "I swiftly scribbled": Cohn, *McCarthy*, 203.

163 "Knowing that": The following exchange between McCarthy and Welch is from *Army-McCarthy Hearings*, 2427–29 (June 9, 1954).

165 "What did I do?": Straight, *Trial by Television*, 253.

McCARTHY'S CENSURE AND HIS END

166 "I think they should get": C. P. Trussell, "Flanders Moves in Senate to Strip McCarthy of Posts," *New York Times*, June 12, 1954, quoted in Oshinsky, *Conspiracy So Immense*, 466.

166 "You're the kid": Cohn, *McCarthy*, 224.

167 "The McCarthy case had been": Floyd M. Riddick, interview by Donald A. Ritchie, October 18, 1978, transcript, 344, Oral History Project, Senate Historical Office, senate.gov/artandhistory/history/oral_history/Floyd_M_Riddick.htm.

168 "The controversy is": William S. White, "M'Carthy as a Martyr Big Problem for G.O.P.," *New York Times*, November 14, 1954.

168 "Last night I had": Beverly Smith, "The Job No Senator Wanted," *Saturday Evening Post*, November 13, 1954, 26.

168   "I intend to run": Arthur V. Watkins, *Enough Rope: The Inside Story of the Censure of Senator Joe McCarthy by His Colleagues* (Englewood Cliffs, NJ: Prentice-Hall, 1969), 197.

168   "It was funny": Smith, "Job No Senator Wanted"; Stewart Alsop to Senator Atkins, November 17, 1954, in Atkins, *Enough Rope*, 197.

169   "This was the very room": The description of the proceedings and the exchange between McCarthy and Watkins are from Smith, "Job No Senator Wanted," 27; see also *Hearings on S. Res. 301: Hearings Before a Select Committee to Study Censure Charges, United States Senate*, 83rd Cong., 38 (August 31, 1954).

169   "The only similarity": James Reston, "Point of Order Becomes Out of Order," *New York Times*, September 1, 1954.

170   "Frankly, I think": Riddick oral history, Senate Historical Office, 374.

170   "Perhaps the most widely": William S. White, "What Motivates Joseph McCarthy," *New York Times Magazine*, March 21, 1954, 55.

171   "This is what": Francis O. Wilcox, interview by Donald A. Ritchie, March 21, 1984, transcript, 114, Oral History Project, Senate Historical Office, senate.gov /artandhistory/history/oral_history/Francis_O_Wilcox.htm.

171   "After the Senate": Riddick oral history, Senate Historical Office, 369.

171   "After his news value": Wilcox oral history, Senate Historical Office, 105.

172   "By the end of '55": Ruth Young Watt, interview by Donald A. Ritchie, September 21, 1979, transcript, 151, Women of the Senate Oral History Project, Senate Historical Office, senate.gov/artandhistory/history/oral_history/Ruth_Young _Watt.htm.

172   "His rise to fame": "To a Turbulent Spirit: Rest at Last in Peace," editorial, *Courier-Journal* (Louisville, KY), May 4, 1957.

172   "He was a complete patriot": "Senator Joseph R. McCarthy," editorial, *Daily News* (New York), May 4, 1957.

172   "The death of Senator Joseph": "Senator McCarthy Passes," editorial, *Atlanta Journal*, May 3, 1957.

173   "If some of his enemies": "Debate May Last for Years," editorial, *Newark* (NJ) *Star-Ledger*, quoted in *Memorial Services Held in the Senate and House of Representatives of the United States, Together with Remarks Presented in Eulogy of Joseph Raymond*

McCarthy, Late Senator from Wisconsin, 85th Cong., 333 (May 6, 1957) (remarks of Representative Lawrence H. Smith of Wisconsin).

173 "There was a genuine broad recognition": Editorial, *New York Herald Tribune*, quoted in "Editorial Views on McCarthy," *New York Times*, May 4, 1957.

173 "Joe McCarthy was murdered": William Loeb, "Murdered!," editorial, *Manchester (NH) Union Leader*, May 3, 1957.

EPILOGUE: WITCH HUNTS DIDN'T END

174 "My father could finally come back": Josh, interview with authors, July 18, 2018.

175 "He was very consistent": William C. Sullivan, quoted in Tim Weiner, *Enemies: A History of the FBI* (New York: Random House, 2012), 199.

176 "Hoover did not welcome": Taylor Branch, *Parting the Waters: America in the King Years, 1954–63* (New York: Simon & Schuster, 1988), 903.

176 "In the light of King's powerful": William C. Sullivan to A. H. Belmont, memo re "Communist Party USA/Negro Question," August 30, 1963, in Martin Luther King, pt. 2, p. 71, FBI FOIA Vault, quoted in Tim Weiner, *Enemies: A History of the FBI* (New York: Random House, 2012), 235.

176 "My parents were not": Toby Emmer's anecdote about his mother and Mrs. Saskin comes from his interview with the authors, April 1, 2021.

177 "How many Americans lost their jobs": Griffin Fariello, ed., introduction to *Red Scare: Memories of the American Inquisition; An Oral History* (New York: Norton, 1995), 42.

177 "My father died of stomach cancer": Sheila Sampton, interview with authors, April 30, 2018.

178 "Nobody really talked": Robin Bady, interview with the authors, March 20, 2020.

178 "I have two legacies": Josh, interview with authors, July 18, 2018.

179 "In 2006, my daughter started a family club": Toby Emmer, interview with authors, April 1, 2021.

179 "No one trusts"; "That's the way" and "[The killer] said": "The Ordeal," *The Adventures of Robin Hood*, Series 1, Episode 11, screenplay by Ring Lardner Jr. (writing as Eric Heath), 1955, dailymotion.com/video/x3djk5r.

179 "The sheriff thought": "The Alchemist," *The Adventures of Robin Hood*, Series 1,

Episode 15, screenplay by Ring Lardner Jr. (writing as Eric Heath), 1956, daily motion.com/video/xxnuta.

179 "Don't be afraid to go into your libraries": Dwight D. Eisenhower, remarks at the Dartmouth College commencement, June 14, 1953, in *Public Papers of the Presidents: Dwight D. Eisenhower, 1953* (Washington, D.C.: U.S. Government Printing Office, 1960), 411.

FURTHER READING

Bayley, Edwin R. *Joe McCarthy and the Press*. Madison: University of Wisconsin Press, 1981.

Brimner, Larry Dane. *Blacklisted! Hollywood, the Cold War, and the First Amendment*. Honesdale, PA: Calkins Creek, 2018.

Charles, Douglas M. *Hoover's War on Gays: Exposing the FBI's "Sex Deviates" Program*. Lawrence: University Press of Kansas, 2015.

Cohn, Roy. *McCarthy*. New York: Lancer Books, 1968.

Evans, Stanton. *Blacklisted by History: The Untold Story of Senator Joe McCarthy and His Fight Against America's Enemies*. New York: Crown Forum, 2007. (This source has been criticized by many historians; it is a defense of McCarthy.)

Fried, Albert, ed. *McCarthyism and the Great American Red Scare: A Documentary History*. New York: Oxford University Press, 1997.

Fried, Richard, M. *Nightmare in Red: The McCarthy Era in Perspective*. New York: Oxford University Press, 1990.

Giblin, James Cross. *The Rise and Fall of Senator Joe McCarthy*. Boston: Clarion Books, 2009.

Halberstam, David. *The Fifties*. New York: Ballantine Books, 1994.

Herman, Arthur. *Joseph McCarthy: Reexamining the Life and Legacy of America's Most Hated Senator*. New York: Free Press, 2000.

Immell, Myra, ed. *Perspectives on Modern World History: The McCarthy Era*. Detroit: Greenhaven Press, 2011.

Johnson, David K. *The Lavender Scare: The Cold War Persecutions of Gays and Lesbians in the Federal Government*. Chicago: University of Chicago Press, 2004.

Korean War Legacy Foundation. *The Korean War and Its Legacy: Teaching About Korea Through Inquiry*. Silver Spring, MD: National Council for the Social Studies, 2019.

Morgan, Ted. *Reds: McCarthyism in Twentieth-Century America*. New York: Random House, 2003.

Oshinsky, David M. *A Conspiracy So Immense: The World of Joe McCarthy*. New York: Free Press, 1983.

Reeves, Thomas C. *The Life and Times of Joe McCarthy: A Biography*. New York: Stein and Day, 1982.

Rovere, Richard. *Senator Joe McCarthy*. New York: Harcourt Brace, 1959.

Sbardellati, John. *J. Edgar Hoover Goes to the Movies: The FBI and the Origins of Hollywood's Cold War*. Ithaca: Cornell University Press, 2012.

Schrecker, Ellen. *Many Are the Crimes: McCarthyism in America*. Princeton, NJ: Princeton University Press, 1998.

Sheinkin, Steve. *Bomb: The Race to Build—and Steal—the World's Most Dangerous Weapon*. New York: Roaring Brook Press, 2012.

Theoharis, Athan, ed. *From the Secret Files of J. Edgar Hoover*. Chicago: Ivan R. Dee, 1991.

Tye, Larry. *Demagogue: The Life and Long Shadow of Senator Joe McCarthy*. New York: Houghton Mifflin Harcourt, 2020.

ACKNOWLEDGMENTS

We wanted to acknowledge the generosity of spirit of the many people who shared their memories with us for this book, both named and unnamed. History damages real people, and these folks bravely revealed the confusion they felt as children and young adults during the McCarthy era. We wrote this book for them, to ensure that their memories are part of history.

Emily Feinberg, our editor at Roaring Brook, has an immediate and instinctive understanding of why we wanted to do our book this way and helped us make meaningful and deep-rooted connections—even though Covid meant we had to do without as many snacks. Emilia Sowersby provided a wonderful additional perspective and helped us see things we had missed.

Jodi Reamer, our agent, understood from the beginning our commitment to telling history in a way that combines primary sources and humor.

Tim Foley's wonderful illustrations bring the period to life.

We want to thank this book's designer, L. Whitt, and art director,

Mallory Grigg, for the magnificent job they did with both the cover and the interior.

Once again, we needed a heroic copyediting and production team. Our thanks to Roaring Brook's Jennifer Healey and John Nora; proofreader Janet Renard; and our own copyediting goddess, Ellen Balis.

We thank the librarians at John Jay College, especially Kathleen Collins.

Our thanks to the Bank Street Children's Book Committee, which taught us so much about the importance of how to write and source twenty-first-century nonfiction.

To our friends and fellow authors who read, listened, and shared our passion for telling this story and our awareness it could happen again: Lucy Frank, Theodora Skipitares, Linda Brossel, Patty Lakin, Roxanne Orgill, Susan Kuklin, Annissa Helie, Melania Clavell, Alison Kavey, Robie Harris, Nan Bases, Itai Sneh, David Munns, and Larry and Margaret Pine.

And to our families—George Harris, Jesse Balis Harris, Sofie Balis Harris, Caitlin Millat, Larry and Peggy Levy, Dana and Pat Kirby, and Erica Levy Ringel and Paul Ringel—who not only supported us but give us hope for the twenty-first century.

INDEX